THE RITZ
OF PARIS

THE RITZ
OF PARIS

STEPHEN WATTS

W · W · NORTON & COMPANY · INC ·
NEW YORK

Jan., 1965

ACKNOWLEDGMENTS

Acknowledgment is gratefully made to the authors and publishers of a number of books to which I have referred or from which, with permission, I have quoted. These include :

What Became of Anna Bolton by Louis Bromfield
Gentlemen Prefer Blondes by Anita Loos
Some People by Harold Nicolson
The Quest for Proust by André Maurois
Paris After Dark by Art Buchwald
Scott Fitzgerald by Andrew Turnbull
Assignment to Catastrophe by Major-General
      Sir Edward L. Spears
The Veiled Wanderer by Princess Marthe Bibesco
The History of Champagne by André L. Simon
Elegant Wits and Grand Horizontals by Cornelia
      Otis Skinner
Nostalgia—A Psychological Study of Marcel Proust by
      Milton L. Miller
The Artistry of Mixing Drinks by Frank Meier
A Fly Fisher's Life by Charles Ritz

and—of course—

César Ritz, Host to the World by Marie-Louise Ritz

S.W.

CONTENTS

ILLUSTRATIONS

THE RITZ
OF PARIS

PROLOGUE

IT COULD be argued that Ritz is the only four-letter word in demotic English that can be said or printed in any civilised country not only with propriety and impunity but with the confident expectation of conveying a distinct and evocative meaning. It is unarguably the only hotel name which has passed into common usage in many languages, dropped its capitalised initial, become a noun, spawned an adjective, and found its way into most English-language dictionaries.

Yet its source is simply the surname of a man—César Ritz— who was alive within the lifetime of anybody now aged forty-five or more; a man who never made a million or a movie, who would have gone unrecognised in the street by all but a minutely fractional percentage of the population of the two cities, Paris and London, where most of his working life was spent.

Even quite reasonably educated and sophisticated people are often surprised—and I have conducted a casual but illuminating spot-poll on this point over the last year or so—to realise that when they say 'ritz' or 'ritzy' they are using a man's name; that 'jones' or 'jonesy' would be an exact if unlikely parallel. I have known people to confess that they thought the adjective came first and the hotel name derived from it. Madame Marie-Louise Ritz, César's widow, who died only two years ago, once overheard an American girl say, as she paused in the lobby of the Paris Ritz and looked at the inconspicuous plaque to the founder's memory, 'I can't believe there was a *man* called Ritz. I mean, it's just a *word*, isn't it? You know, chic . . . de luxe . . . swell.'

[9]

Perhaps the definitive and perfect combination of name and word in one sentence was achieved, quite spontaneously, some years ago by César's son, Charles Ritz, when talking with American travel agents who admitted that they sometimes hesitated to send their customers to the Paris Ritz because they might think it 'too grand' for them. 'The Ritz,' declared Ritz *fils* memorably, 'is *not* ritzy.'

Ritz with a capital 'r' is well and widely spattered about the world too. 'Children of the Ritz', 'Puttin' on the Ritz', 'The Diamond as Big as the Ritz', 'Charles of the Ritz' (no connection with César's son mentioned above), 'Ritz Theatre', 'Ritz Crackers'—songs, fiction, cosmetics, cinema, biscuits; and nobody doubts that, whatever the context, the sense intended to be conveyed is of style, luxury, elegance, grandeur or top quality.

As a surname Ritz is by no means common. The telephone directories of London, Manhattan and Paris yield a total of only fourteen individuals bearing the name; but New York City has twenty-four commercial enterprises trading under the name of Ritz and in London there are thirty-seven companies registered in the name of Ritz, only two of them having anything to do with hotels. Theatres, ballrooms, restaurants (including snack bars and a fish-and-chip shop), pharmacies, engineers, fabric merchants, makers of shirts, flooring, paper boxes and baby carriages have chosen Ritz for their business titles. (The oddest and most contradictory is the Ritz Thrift Shop in New York, which specialises in furs.)

And none of this proliferation would have happened but for a Swiss peasant's son who once herded his father's goats, who became a waiter and then an hotel manager, who built up over the hard-working years a dream of the ideal hotel, and, when he was forty-eight, fulfilled his dream and opened the Hotel Ritz in the Place Vendôme in Paris—'a little house,' he said, 'to which I am very proud to see my name attached'.

How the 'little house' in Paris came to be; what it is like today; the man who made it and those who came after him; and how the name Ritz came to mean what it does—these are the subject of this book.

CHAPTER ONE

THE HOTEL

THE HOTEL idea is as old as man on the move. The ancient traveller who rigged up a primitive tent and lit a fire for warmth and cooking and to keep the more treacherous fauna at bay was dealing with the essence of the matter on a do-it-yourself basis. His needs were shelter and safety: a place to stop, eat and sleep.

The notion of somebody else providing these facilities for payment followed naturally. The biblical inn was at first an enclosed courtyard and then a public building for the Asiatic wayfarer. The Persians called a group of travellers a *karwan*, or caravan, and in the same language *sarai* was a big house; simple addition provides our word caravanserai, which Webster still gives as a synonym for hotel.

By the Middle Ages the travellers' rest was recognisably an hotel, with 'a sign, a host, a staff of servants, a *table d'hôte* meal and a reckoning'. Comfort and hygiene came earlier into the picture than might be expected, for by 1577 the Reverend William Harrison was writing in his *Description of England* of 'sumptuous innes ... very well furnished with naperie. ... Each commer is due to lie in cleane sheets wherein no man hath beene lodged since they came from the laundresse.'

The Latin *hospes* means a host or a guest, so a hospice (or hospital) was a place where a host received guests, where 'hospitality' was offered. *Hospes* became *hoste* in Old French, *hôte* in modern French and 'host' in English; hence 'hotel' and 'hostel'. As methods of transport increased and commerce grew, hotels ceased to be confined to the main highways; they spread to the towns, the rail terminals, seaports and resorts. The hotel idea had expanded as to location and clientele, and the only major development to follow was in grandeur. (In recent times, of course, there has been one more trend. With rising site values, grandeur has tended to be sacrificed to economically used cubic footage.)

But in the realm of the grand hotel, which is still very much with us and commands a prestige, affection, even awe, with which the merely functional can never compete, the original Hotel Ritz in Paris—*the* Ritz, by general consent—occupies a towering and almost legendary position.

* * *

The Ritz is not by a long way the biggest hotel in the world, nor is it the grandest or the most expensive, and it is far from being the most venerable. César Ritz opened its doors with pride and trepidation only a little over sixty years ago. And it is equally far from being the most modern; television is unknown to it and radio is forbidden lest anybody should object. The hotel's advertising expenditure in its entire history would be regarded by Madison Avenue as derisory for one year.

Yet the Ritz is probably the best-known hotel in the world and a substantial number of intelligent, fastidious, almost mystically devoted people will tell you simply and firmly that it is the best. If this judgment is contested they may back down to saying that it is their favourite hotel, or at least the only hotel in Paris they would consider staying at.

Like Rolls-Royce in the automobile world, Ritz has become a brand name on so rarefied a level as to be considered above and beyond mere publicity. Writers in newspapers and television, for instance, can often use 'Rolls' or 'Ritz' where any other proprietary name in the same fields would be struck out as inadmissible free advertising.

When Charles Ritz declared, 'The Ritz is *not* ritzy' he was

well aware of the effectiveness of his paradox, but he seriously
meant what he said; in his opinion the popular usage of 'ritzy'
has a distinct overtone of what the English might call 'side'
—of snobbery and ostentation—whereas his father had a hatred
of false pride or condescension, and for all his passion for elegance, and contempt for the cost of it, he never for a moment
forgot that he was the servant of his public (Mme Ritz has even
credited him, wrongly I think, with coining the phrase 'the
customer is always right') and that the function of an hotel is to
provide comfort, refreshment and service.

Indeed, the only snobbery in his attitude was that he aimed
at a class of guest to whom the Ritz would be just like home.
His successors have striven to maintain this tradition and his
son is as likely to criticise empty grandeur for grandeur's sake
as he is quick to detect, in an hotel or restaurant, any other fault
born of pomposity or pretentiousness.

But it is undeniable that the name Ritz has taken on connota-
tions of size and splendour which César would have deplored.
Scott Fitzgerald called one of his short stories 'The Diamond
as Big as the Ritz'; as the gem of his fantasy was a mountain it
would perhaps have been more apposite to say 'A Diamond as
Big as the Waldorf Astoria', but somehow that would not have
been right.

The link between diamonds and the Ritz as symbols of riches
and magnificence recurs elsewhere. In *Gentlemen Prefer Blondes*
Anita Loos's Lorelei had only two criteria, two standards of
value-judgments—diamonds and the Ritz. She decided, it will be
recalled, that American gentlemen were the best 'because kissing
your hand may make you feel very very good but a diamond and
safire bracelet lasts forever'. And 'Ritz' summarised for her the
way of life to which she was determined to adhere. Whether she
was in New York, London, Paris or Budapest, she wrote 'Ritz'
as naturally as some of us would write 'home'. (Of this, at least,
César would have approved; but what would he have thought of
those pick-ups in the lobby?)

She was 'intreeged' and could 'hardly wait to see the Ritz
hotel in Paris'. She found both Paris and the Ritz 'devine':

'So we came to the Ritz Hotel and the Ritz Hotel is devine. Because when a girl can sit in a delightful bar and have delicious champagne cocktails and look at all the important French people in Paris, I think it is devine. I mean when a girl can sit there and look at the Dolly sisters and Pearl White and Maybelle Gilman Corey and Mrs Nash, it is beyond worlds.'

Louis Bromfield's novel about France under the occupation of 1940–4, *What Became of Anna Bolton*, introduces the name Ritz more than a hundred times in 160 pages. The barrage begins slowly with a mere sixteen Ritzes in the first fifty-nine pages, but on page 60 the author introduces Mme Ritz as a character (Anna Bolton gets a lot of sage advice from the old lady in her top-floor apartment of the hotel) and the incidence of Ritz inevitably accelerates. (Employing a curious version of artistic licence, Bromfield killed Mme Ritz off on page 137, during the occupation and seventeen years before her actual demise. Mme Ritz was furious.)

*   *   *

It is possible that a stranger carrying a mental image of the Ritz as the ultimate in grand hotels might be disappointed by a first sight of it. Its frontage on the Place Vendôme, elegant and beautifully proportioned as any part of that magnificent and indeed unique square* must be, is little bigger than many a Parisian one-family town house of patrician days—which it originally was. Over the four arches of the entrance is the only announcement of its presence: three words—'HOTEL' on one side, 'RITZ' in the middle and 'RESTAURANT' on the other, the letters formed by plain, uncoloured electric bulbs standing less than two feet high and never lit up. The shallow, half-elliptical driveway through the extreme arches to the single revolving door is not more than two Cadillac-lengths.

Inside, the hotel is relatively small as hotels go, though it is spacious and high-ceilinged; there are 210 rooms with a capacity

---

* It is, in fact, an octagon, and the façades were completed first, as an entity, then the houses built on behind.

of 230 guests. Absolute capacity is touched only about thirty days in the year, and three-quarters of the year's bookings are concentrated in the periods April–June and September–October. In addition to the bedrooms and suites there are two restaurants and three bars; a tapestry-hung, chandeliered private room of particular elegance—the Salon Carré, which is classified as a national monument by the Ministry of Beaux Arts and cannot be altered without official permission—where private luncheons and dinners may be given; a *salon de thé*, which is on the way to the hotel restaurant and is also used for receptions; and one or two small reading, writing or waiting rooms; but very deliberately there is nothing known as a 'lounge'. ('To avoid undesirable presences', M. Auzello, the managing director, explained to me.)

The interior geography of the hotel is complicated by the fact that it is composed of three buildings—the original No. 15 Place Vendôme which César Ritz bought, with its gardens and stables, and which he extended in depth as far as he could, until it abuts on the property of the next-door neighbour, the Ministry of Justice; No. 17 Place Vendôme, the neighbouring house on the other side, which was bought sixteen years later; and a building in the next street, No. 38 Rue Cambon, which was opened shortly before the First World War and is linked to the Vendôme side of the hotel only by a long passage on the ground floor.

Joseph Wechsberg has described the present-day Ritz as 'a small village consisting of three hotels and a couple of extra buildings, of flower-beds and gardens, terraces and corridors, pavilions and halls, held together by that intangible, impeccable condition known as "Ritz service", by the devotion of its personnel, the pride of its management and the love of its faithful guests . . . an oasis of peace and a haven of tranquillity in the very heart of Paris'. Mr Wechsberg exaggerates the complications a little, but it is certainly true that in an age of monolithic hotel architecture the Ritz is defiantly eccentric, not only in its far from symmetrical ground-plan but also vertically.

No. 15 is a three-storey house with attics; the extension running back along the restaurant-garden has five floors; No. 17, while

apparently matching No. 15 on the front, has one section four
floors high, another of only two floors, and where it surrounds a
small garden, the Petit Jardin Nord, it goes up to five storeys.
All of the Rue Cambon building is six floors high. The floor
levels of these agglomerated buildings vary and short flights of
steps connect one section with another. An incidental conse-
quence of this is that a more than economic number of floor waiters
has to be employed, as no one man's territory may include steps
which are unnegotiable for a wheeled table or trolley.

*   *   *

It is unlikely that any hotel of equal size is so easy to get lost in,
for the growth around the nucleus of No. 15 (the original hotel
was half the size of the present one) tends to be labyrinthine,
and the Ritz does not like staring directional signs which might
give the impression of pandering to strangers. (M. Auzello has
been known to refer to non-residents as 'exterior people'.)

To reach the largest and most celebrated of the three Ritz Bars
from the Vendôme, or front, entrance, for instance, you walk
through the lobby and the *salon de thé* and then, on the threshold
of the dining-room, make a sharp right-hand turn, then a left,
into the long *galerie*, or corridor, lined with glittering showcases. Charles Ritz, meaning only to be helpful, once proposed
to put up a notice at the turning, with an arrow and some such
inscription as: 'Bar'. M. Auzello reacted in horror. 'If such a
notice were put up,' he said, 'I should not sleep for a week.' The
notice has never gone up and it is still a useful ploy of Ritzman-
ship to steer your floundering guest gently round the double
bend, demonstrating that the whole thing is perfectly simple if
you know your Ritz.

Having made the passage of the *vitrines*, you arrive not at the
bar but at a foyer, with some sofas and chairs about, and the
entrance to the grill-room, L'Espadon. The unescorted stranger
(who should perhaps never have essayed the journey anyhow)
sees ahead the *concierge* and reception desk of the Cambon side
and, beyond, the street. But, in fact, just before he reaches the
revolving door, fearing ejection by the page boy eagerly waiting

to swing it for him, there lies, on the right, one of the most famous bars in the world.

* * *

Unlike most hotels nowadays, the Ritz does not use the telephone for floor service. Each room has, on a bedside table, a small battery of buttons marked Chambermaid, Valet, Waiter and *Service Privé*. The first three mean just what they say, but the *Service Privé* button sometimes puzzles guests and a casual push on it will produce nothing, but that does not mean the service does not exist. If you arrive at the Ritz with your own servant the *Service Privé* button in your room will be linked up with a bell in your servant's room. Inevitably the demand for this service is less now that it once was. M. Auzello recalls the time when it was not unusual for one couple to be accompanied by maid, chauffeur, valet and perhaps butler. It was sometimes necessary to rent accommodation in hotels near by when the eighty servants' rooms were all occupied. Now at the height of the season it is rare for forty private servants to be in residence at once.

* * *

There is one suite in the hotel, however, where no liaison by push-button between employer and servant is required, for the servants' quarters—three rooms on a gallery in the entrance hall—are built in. This first-floor suite on the Vendôme side has an imposing double front door alongside which there is a small door, and by this the servants can enter and reach their rooms without going through the hall.

The complex of rooms of which this suite is part was once let as a whole, surely as magnificent a unit of hotel accommodation as there has ever been. It comprised two salons, three double bedrooms, three single bedrooms and four bathrooms. The principal salon is a stately room decorated in Empire style and its stucco murals of the Napoleonic-Egyptian period, depicting scenes from Bonaparte's Egyptian campaign, have been classified as national monuments by the Ministry of Beaux Arts. Gilt sphinxes decorate the fireplace and furniture.

The suite, as now let, consists of this salon with two bedrooms on one side and one on the other. It was here that Göring made his headquarters when he stayed in the hotel during the war, and it is all too easy to imagine him revelling in its massive magnificence.

Two of the smaller rooms of the original suite were transformed by Mme Ritz into an oak-panelled miniature suite for one person, and in contrast with the surrounding rooms it is now a quiet, cosy apartment for which there is constant competition among solo Ritz regulars. Considering its charm and comfort—the atmosphere is that of a secluded bachelor flat, with nothing 'hotel' about it—its cost, at 160 francs a day (less than £12) is relatively low.

At the other end of the scale there is a three-room suite near by, occupying half the Vendôme frontage on the first floor, which was for years retained by Barbara Hutton whether she was in Paris or not. This costs 590 francs a day, which represents a bill of about £300 a week, exclusive of the service charge of fifteen per cent and taxes amounting to another ten per cent, before the occupant has so much as rung for *petit déjeuner* and the morning paper. Overhead, on the second floor, there is a suite much favoured by the Duke and Duchess of Windsor, a less formal apartment, decorated in pink, which lets at 540 francs a day, or a basic £270 a week.

The grand suites now let to a relatively small group of people drawn from very different walks of life—the King and Queen of Greece, the Queen Mother of Jordan, M. Boissvoin, the New York antique dealer, Mr Douglas Dillon, the U.S. Secretary of the Treasury (and former Ambassador to France) and Mr Charles Wrightsman, the Texan oil millionaire, are examples of this select clientele.

On the other hand, the Ritz price range is wider than might be expected. It is possible to have a room for 75 francs (little more than £5) a day, though there are only eight such rooms. The average single room runs about 80–100 francs a day (£6–£7 10s.), double rooms 120–150 francs (£9–£11 10s.) a day and suites for two, other than the regal accommodation already mentioned, from 200–280 francs (£15–£20).

M. Zembrzuski, the resident manager, does not hesitate to say that on strictly economic grounds all the room prices should be higher, but after only fifteen years in Ritz service he recognises that he is something of a new boy and he doubts if he can ever persuade his superiors, who are stubbornly reluctant to increase charges and have even been known, for purely sentimental reasons, to charge an old client almost the same as he paid on his first visit, even though that may have been years ago.

Confronted with such whimsical and unorthodox attitudes to economics, M. Zembrzuski smiles ruefully and mildly says, 'We are not always absolutely commercial. Indeed we do some things here that make nonsense commercially.' But he is a Ritz man and he says it with understanding affection.

M. Zembrzuski was saying something of this sort to me one day when he was showing me over one of the grander suites, and to illustrate his point he indicated the switch he had just turned to light the great chandelier in the salon. Every time the need arises to replace one of these switches M. Zembrzuski shudders a little, for they are made of filigree bronze; they are craft not mass productions, and the craftsmen are vanishing, quite apart from the costs increasing. But the switches are as they have always been since César Ritz selected the design; they are part of the Ritz, so they must remain.

I came across an even more surprising instance of 'commercial nonsense' one day when I was in the tiny office in the cellars which is the headquarters of Maurice, the *chef des caves*. There is an 1812 cognac listed as 'Grande Fine Ritz Reserve' which, Maurice remarked in passing, they 'give away'. Twice or three times a year, when an old customer gives a party or reception, this brandy is served and charged at fifteen francs a glass. A bottle provides fifteen glasses, so the Ritz takes 225 francs (or £16) for a bottle of a cognac for which they have been offered £25 and more a bottle. But the Ritz argument is that there is little virtue in making a cash profit on a small stock when, so long as it lasts, their friends who appreciate it can have it at a price a sensible man is prepared to pay.

What is particularly endearing about Ritz eccentricities is that

[19]

they are entirely unselfconscious; there is no cult of idiosyncrasy or of old-worldliness, and far from making capital out of the quirks that have become traditions the hotel personnel yield up information about them casually or sometimes even reluctantly. I have often encountered genuine surprise when inquiring about something which struck me as odd. For example, one does not have to be a time-and-motion student to notice that the chain of executive communication is, to say the least, winding. (Indeed a time-and-motion man would surely throw up his hands in despair.) Normal telephonic inter-communication is used, of course, but in something so personal as an hotel a good deal of man-to-man consultation is involved.

M. Ritz, the president (or chairman of the board), has no office at all. He lives at the top of the hotel and covers many miles a day, at a sharp, almost trotting pace. M. Auzello works in a small, uncarpeted and somewhat cluttered room off a minor lounge close by the Vendôme entrance. It was originally a writing-room, but M. Auzello transformed it into his office on a whim one day when he decided he was tired of climbing stairs (on account of having had frostbitten feet in the First World War) and he has remained there ever since.

M. Zembrzuski occupies the office on the gallery over the Vendôme doorway, which was previously M. Auzello's. He has not yet complained about the stair-climbing, but he is nearly a quarter of a century younger than M. Auzello. M. Penché, the young secretary-general, who has to be in constant touch with M. Auzello, has a modern but distinctly cramped first-floor office on the Cambon side, some four minutes' smart walk away and reached by an iron-railed stone stair leading up from the staff entrance. Another director, Mr W. H. Taylor, an English accountant who arrived on a temporary assignment from his London employers forty years ago and was secretary-general until his retirement five years ago, continues to operate from a first-floor converted bedroom on the Rue Cambon where, with a reach of the hand into a cupboard, he can produce copperplate minutes of board meetings or menus for special dinners of half a century ago.

This dispersal of executives worries nobody unduly and indeed is not entirely accidental. That the top echelon administration should have to walk about a bit in the course of the day's work means that they can oversee a multitude of details and (if they wish) meet the guests, and this is important in the Ritz tradition of hotel-keeping. For example, in walking the eighty-yard corridor from one side of the hotel to the other M. Auzello or M. Ritz is able to make a quick, keen review of the hundred-odd *vitrines*, or showcases, and satisfy himself that they are as immaculate as they ought to be. These *vitrines* are a feature of the Ritz and many women arriving to keep an appointment in the bar (on the Cambon side) will deliberatively enter from the Place Vendôme in order to enjoy ten minutes of the most attractive and concentrated window-shopping Paris can offer.

This glittering gallery demonstrates in a small way César Ritz's genius for making a virtue of a necessity. When the Cambon building was added to the hotel the management had to face the fact that a long corridor was unavoidable. What could be done with it? Ritz by then had been an invalid for years, but still it was he who provided the answer: 'Place beautiful things there.' Leading Paris shops, carefully selected, should be invited to display their goods in elegant showcases—naturally under the artistic control of the hotel. This would provide suitable decoration and at the same time make the walk seem shorter.

At first it was not intended to charge—the arrangement would be based simply on mutual benefit. But the response of the shopkeepers was such that a rental system was instituted and the *vitrines*, still carefully supervised as to content and style, now yield the Ritz a substantial income. The showcase arcade idea has been copied by hotels all over the world.

There is even a practical benefit in the fact that Charles Ritz has no office, far less executive suite. He keeps his appointments in one or other of the public rooms and nothing escapes his eye, as when, not long ago, meeting me in the Cambon lobby, he spotted a burn about the size of a pin-head on a sofa and had given instructions for its repair before we began our conversation.

[21]

When I mentioned the somewhat diffused office arrangements M. Ritz cocked an eyebrow and gently suggested that perhaps speed is something that can be overdone. 'Not everything is better because it is done like lightning,' he said. 'In that way things can become standardised. We like to remain individual.'

*　　*　　*

M. Ritz has been an enthusiastic fisherman all his life and makes the deadpan claim that his twelve years' residence in America stemmed from an offer of an hotel job in Connecticut which he accepted because he thought it would be handy for Canada, where he had been told the fishing was good. The recent transformation of the Ritz's grill-room into the now flourishing L'Espadon (swordfish), specialising in sea-food dishes, can be directly traced to his piscatorial influence.

In L'Espadon he was determined to create a décor which would suggest outdoors, with a lowered, sky-like ceiling, and pillars of variegated granite chips which he went to Italy to find and select, as to colour, himself. Another of his details was the introduction of Venetian glass for the service of shellfish and special dishes to hold nine oysters for the man who cannot quite decide between a dozen and a half-dozen.

Acknowledging the fact that the American proportion of Ritz custom has in the post-war years risen to nearly fifty per cent, he made a tour a few years ago from which he was determined to return with the answer to the important question: what does the American visitor to the Ritz want—and what will he or she want five years from now? Instead of coming back to M. Auzello and the board with a complicated report, M. Charles decided the answer lay in one word: contrast. By this, he explains, he meant that in his view the Ritz-bound American did not want an American hotel. The American who wanted that did not have to cross the ocean. Thus the decoration and furnishing of Ritz rooms should be kept traditional.

But he also decided that the worst feature of American hotel life was room service. So the Ritz service in this department should be kept to the highest possible round-the-clock level.

On the other hand, Americans did not look for or cherish old-world standards in the purely functional departments. Thus there should be concentration on the modernisation of bath-rooms. Even this should be subject to modification: while Ritz bathrooms should have well-lit mirrors at the right height, showers, hair-washing facilities and universal points for electric razors, there would be no such excesses as strip lighting, and a sufficient degree of traditional character (and contrast) would be preserved by the size of the bathrooms (his father thought a bathroom should always be a *room*) and the height of the ceilings.

Basically the economic operation of all hotels is the same; it is simple, and very much like the budgetary problem every house-wife knows: on a given but often variable income you maintain a house, pay the servants if you have any, buy food, cook it, serve it, and give as much attention as possible to the personal well-being of the people under your roof. It is only in scale and style and service that an hotel can differ from a home, or from another hotel. There are hotels which are 'personal' and many more which are impersonal. The Ritz, for all its implications of grandeur, has always sought to be as home-like as possible, to regard guests as really guests and not just cash customers. César Ritz often referred to the Ritz as his 'house' and in his diary he once wrote, 'In no trade is the relationship between buyer and seller so close and intimate as that between client and proprietor of an hotel.'

If a strictly economic policy were applied, the problems would be fewer; it is when taste and tradition and an almost obsessive concern about detail come in that the equilibrium is more diffi-cult to maintain. The Ritz derives ninety-six per cent of its in-come from selling accommodation and refreshment (food and drink), but on the expenditure side there is no such fixity: this is where 'commercial nonsense' creeps in. To cite two examples: maintenance should mean economically that a worn chair be re-covered in a suitable material; at the Ritz it means re-covering it in the material César Ritz originally chose and which the management believe their customers 'expect', notwithstanding the fact that the material is hard to get nowadays and very expensive. The provision of wood-burning fires in all rooms would seem to represent a heavy expense in an hotel which has central heating throughout; the answer is that they are a Ritz tradition.

There are many other examples of a deep-seated resistance to change, except in purely functional modernisation. The same attitude extends to the staff. Much of the 'personal touch' in an hotel must come from the servants and therefore the Ritz cherishes its old staff. This can, of course, present problems. One such arose not long ago when the hotel's seventy-five-year-old chief plumber issued a 'keep out' edict from his basement workshop; he would not allow anyone to enter or touch anything. The root of the trouble was that the workshop had become a glory-hole of the accumulated paraphernalia of plumbing for half a century; to the plumber it was all perfectly satisfactory, but to anybody else it was chaos. When a fitment, even a washer, was needed for a repair the assistant plumbers often could not find it, and it was discovered that they were going out and buying what they needed, which caused delays infuriating to both guests and management.

It was clear that if the old man was ordered any further he would quit, an alarming thought for one reason if no other: the water-pipe system of the hotel has been altered and added to over the years and, as work on bathroom renovation is constantly going on, it is essential to have someone with a detailed knowledge of this leaden maze hidden behind walls and tiles. And the old man was the only possessor of this knowledge.

M. Ritz asked him to come and see him. He arrived, respectful but stubbornly muttering about the time having come for him to retire. The chairman explained that he was not just a member of the staff, he 'belonged to the house' and so far as the management were concerned he was welcome to stay as long as he liked. But what they all wanted (did they not?) was that the Ritz should be efficient, giving the best service in all departments. So, as a favour, would he allow them to give him help to reorganise his workshop? After all, it would not be in the tradition if a service fell down because only one man knew where things were kept.

The old man agreed and felt happy that he had done 'the house' a personal favour.

The case of the veteran plumber is an extreme example of an attitude not uncommon at the Ritz; the staff tend to be quite as resistant to change as the most conservative guest. Charles Ritz cites as another instance of this the occasion when a potato-frying machine was introduced into the kitchens. He is not entirely sure what happened, but the machine was out and back at the makers in remarkably quick time. It took two years of subtle campaigning and propaganda before the machine was brought back, installed and accepted. 'They don't take to anything new the first time,' he says. 'They make you feel you're trying to change the text of the Bible.'

Sometimes the right psychological approach to achieve the desired end is not by means of asking favours. M. Auzello dealt with a situation not long ago where sharp, direct action was required to maintain 'Ritz standards'. An important New York business man, who always stays at the hotel when in Paris, was reported going around without either a coat or a tie. In fact, he had come in from playing golf and was in a sports shirt. M. Auzello tackled the man at once in tones of polite reproach. 'You, Mr Blank,' he said, 'a very big man and an esteemed client of the Ritz—setting a bad example!' The guest accepted the rebuke meekly and never sinned again.

A notice was put up at the entrances: 'Gentlemen circulating in this hotel are kindly requested to wear jacket and tie.' Far from offence being taken, M. Auzello says, he was congratulated by many American visitors on taking this stand, 'showing', he adds, 'their desire to see good standards maintained'.

Dignity and commerce, pride and salesmanship, have some-times to be combined if an hotel is to survive, and the Ritz has had to discard occasionally the gracious illusion that its host-and-guest relationship is on a non-mercenary basis. After the Wall Street disaster of 1929, for instance, there was a reflected slump in the volume of American patronage of the Ritz, as of Europe in general. In the early Thirties the situation was still bad enough for the Ritz management to feel that it must be conveyed to

Americans that the hotel was not only for the millionaire class, whose ranks were now depleted.

Charles Ritz was the chosen ambassador and he toured twenty cities in thirty days, talking to travel agents and other groups. (It was at this time that M. Ritz coined the phrase, 'The Ritz is not ritzy.') This is probably the most overt selling the Ritz has ever done.

More recently, it was found that while L'Espadon was flourishing, the hotel restaurant was not. This is a common trouble with hotels in cities. Whereas it was once usual to lunch or dine where you were staying, visitors have become steadily more adventurous and increasingly tend to dine out. In Paris, quite apart from the handful of celebrated restaurants which a moneyed visitor may regard as a 'must', there has grown up an inverted snobbism which may be summed up as the 'We know a little bistro' cult. Again the Ritz recognised the need for action and an elegant, crested card was printed and placed in every room.

The Ritz speaking in its collective managerial voice to its customers is worth a little study. The opening sentence does not introduce the subject in hand at all: 'The Management wish to call the attention of guests to the fact that the name 'Ritz' stands for a tradition which for more than half a century has made our hotel famous throughout the world.'

The approach continues oblique, but the tone has just a hint of appeal for sympathy: 'In order to maintain the feeling of privacy, and the personal service and comfort which have always been its special features, a great amount of perseverance and effort is required, especially in these times of extreme standardisation and industrialisation.'

Then, in paragraph three, we sidle up to the main theme: 'Our ideal is also to maintain in our restaurant as perfect a service as possible, and cooking in accordance with the principles laid down by César Ritz and his collaborator, the famous *chef de cuisine* Escoffier, pupils of whom are today still working in our kitchens.'

Then in paragraph four, the penultimate and shortest, the point is introduced with becoming candour, but not by any means hammered home: 'The expense necessary to maintain these traditions is exceedingly high and becoming almost overwhelming.' And finally the message: 'Considering the foregoing, the Management would be most grateful to you if, uniting your efforts with their own, you would do them the honour of taking your meals in our restaurant on the Vendôme side during the time you are staying under our roof.'

Notice how guest-identification with the problems of the hotel, a sense of what, put vulgarly, would be 'we're in this together and if we all pull together we'll win through', is achieved with tact and taste in six words in the middle—'uniting your efforts with their own'.

*　　　*　　　*

Late at night the quiet of the Ritz is cathedral-like, and quiet always suggests placidity and peace. But there are times when this somnolent atmosphere is rudely disturbed and the hotel has to be ready for such emergencies. An hotel man always has to remember that however busy the day has been, however many problems have been met and solved, the most important moment may come at three a.m. when a woman rings down and says her husband is knocking her about. And an hotel man, on the managerial level, develops an intuitive reaction to these sudden, dramatic upsurges. He learns to know when to soothe and when to use drastic measures.

Many years ago there was a Ritz regular who came home in the early hours every morning in a four-wheeler cab and refused to get out. Normal persuasions did not work and there was always the danger of an ugly scene. He was an amiable but stubborn drunk, and there was gradually evolved a nightly dialogue between him and the night porter.

'Who's that up there?' the drunk asked, pointing to the top of the column in the centre of the Place Vendôme.

'Napoleon,' said the night porter.

'Then I'll go to bed when he comes down and shakes hands with me,' said the drunk.

Every night the porter explained that it was not possible for

Napoleon to come down. Every night the drunk listened to the unvarying explanation, nodded understandingly and allowed himself to be led quietly indoors.

A common night-call is from the woman who announces, often hysterically, that she has been robbed. Her jewels have been stolen. Perhaps she has put them somewhere and forgotten? No, she knows where they were and now they are gone. Almost invariably a search of well-known 'safe places' where women hide their jewellery—and then forget they have done so—produces the missing articles. The soap-dish in the bathroom is the favourite place.

Intuition plays a delicately important part in an hotel manager's life; delicate because he dare not ignore his hunches and yet the consequences of putting a foot wrong may be formidable. On one occasion a solo American arrived at the hotel for the first time. He was a perfectly normal, unexceptionable middle-aged man, called (let us say) Stern, but M. Zembrzuski, for no reason he can explain, immediately took a dubious view of him.

After a few days the news came to the managerial ears that Mr Stern was a big spender and his bill was mounting rapidly. M. Zembrzuski was worried, but there was no action he could reasonably take. A day or two later there was a telephone call to the Ritz from a New York travel agent, asking if Mr Stern was staying there. Told that he was, the caller asked when he was leaving. The Ritz did not know. 'He owes money all over the place,' said the travel agent. 'I'm coming over. Detain him.' The call was put through to M. Zembrzuski. 'We cannot detain him,' he said. 'We are not the police.'

The manager thought about the matter for the rest of that day. Then he told the cashier to telephone Mr Stern and ask when he was going. The answer was in two days. M. Zembrzuski had his bill made up, including the two days. It amounted to about a thousand dollars. Then he rang Mr Stern and said he would like to see him. The manager presented himself with the bill in his hand, but behind his back. 'We have had very bad news about your credit,' he said. The guest immediately asked where the information came from. 'I cannot tell you that', said M.

Zembrzuski, 'but we hotel men have our ways.' Mr Stern was very angry and insulted. He blustered. M. Zembrzuski stood firm. 'Sir,' he said, 'I am an employee and I am responsible to my employers. I am naturally very worried.' Mr Stern then became very understanding and sympathetic. He said he would put the manager's fears at rest right away and produced 500 dollars. M. Zembrzuski then produced the bill and suggested it should be paid in full. To his surprise Mr Stern paid up.

But again he asked about the source of the information; this obviously worried him. The manager said it came from New York. That seemed to worry Mr Stern even more. But, he said, Stern was a very common name in New York and obviously he was being confused with some other Stern. 'I hope so,' said M. Zembrzuski, and left, very relieved because his bill was paid.

In the next two days the Stern account was carefully watched. It was not very big and when it was presented he paid and left. He went out of his way to tell M. Zembrzuski that he had arranged for a letter to be sent from a Swiss bank, guaranteeing that his credit was good. The letter never came. It was, incidentally, noted that Mr Stern announced that he was going to London, but in fact he took a plane to Rome.

Sometimes the rich are careless about money matters. If a guest leaves with money owing it is often very difficult to collect it later. Especially difficult is the collection of debts from guests who put items on the bill *after* they have paid it. For example, a very rich and formidable old South American woman stayed at the Ritz for some time. Everybody was frightened of her. She could be very unreasonable. Her bill was large, and she paid it on the morning she was leaving. But she had arranged a large luncheon party that day and the management learned that she was leaving immediately afterwards. The cashier reported anxiously to the manager. 'She'll never pay *another* bill,' he said. 'We cannot present it to her before her guests.' M. Zembrzuski said he would take charge of the matter. He posted himself in the lobby and when the old lady came out from lunch and went straight towards the car that was waiting at the door he approached her, kissed her hand, and produced the bill. She paid it, but the management knew very well that if she had left without doing so the money would never have been recovered.

It is the general experience of hotel men that customers have become steadily 'more human', that is less inclined to treat hotel servants as if they were non-human. There are still, of course, 'bad' clients—people with bad manners or who demand more than is reasonable. They are known among the Ritz staff as '*méchant*'. It says much for the forbearance of the servants that people who make their lives a misery should be described as merely 'naughty'.

* * *

The name 'Ritz' as applied to an hotel is safeguarded, so far as the varying laws of copyright permit, in most countries, but at frequent intervals the promoters of a new hotel feel that it is the only apt name for their child, and they ask the Paris company for permission to use it. The Ritz is not at all stuffy about this; but the management want to be quite sure the hotel is worthy of the name, and they will go to considerable trouble before making a decision.

In one recent case a letter was received from Italy seeking permission to call a new hotel the Ritz. The promoters were enthusiastic; theirs was going to be, they said, 'the ritziest hotel in Europe'. It was not an auspicious start, but M. Auzello and M. Ritz consulted together and it was decided that M. Ritz should go to Italy and look into the project.

After a little conversation he began to doubt if the promoters' practical knowledge of hotel-keeping was equal to their enthusiasm. He began to ask test questions, to study blueprints. He asked about floor service. The Italians said they would have pantries on every floor. M. Ritz said this was what the Ritz used to do, but it was now impossible because of shortage of labour. The only way was to have lifts direct from the kitchens to each floor—each lift being capable of carrying two 'chariots'. In the kitchen the chariots would be laid in advance. The point of having the lifts the right size was that a waiter serving breakfast could serve two rooms with one journey of the lift. People expect breakfast within ten minutes of ordering it, said M. Ritz. Once they would have been content to wait half an hour, but not now.

At last, as their trump card, the Italians announced that they were going to buy an obsolete aircraft-carrier which would be anchored in the harbour in bad weather and outside the three-mile limit in fine weather. This would contain swimming pools, bars, a night-club. . . . M. Ritz rose and prepared to go. 'The Ritz,' he said with absolute finality, 'will not lend its name to an aircraft-carrier.'

CHAPTER TWO

A MAN CALLED RITZ

WHEN THE girl who stopped by César Ritz's modest memorial in the hotel recovered from her surprise that there actually was 'a man called Ritz', she no doubt imagined a patriarchal figure playing host for a lifetime, or at least a generation, within those quietly elegant walls. In fact, one of the most surprising things about the man who not only conceived and created the hotel but put his stamp indelibly upon it for all time is that he presided over it in person for only four years.

But to those who have been in charge of the Ritz during the other sixty years of its existence César Ritz is an ever-present influence rather than a memory. None of them now living ever worked with Ritz. When ill-health, brought on by overwork, forced him to withdraw from active life at the early age of fifty-two, his elder son Charles was a boy of eleven and Claude Auzello too was still at school.

Auzello joined the staff in 1919, after serving in the First World War; Ritz had died the previous year, a few days before the Armistice, having been a tragic invalid for sixteen years. But in any conversation with the present generation the name of César recurs frequently, not so much in awed tones of reverence as in practical terms of maintaining the standards he set, as though they had taken over from him a year or two ago at most. So thoroughly did he imbue those around him with his ideals and purpose that the course he set has been followed undeviatingly through six vastly changing decades of European social history.

The first thing the eye lights on in the managing director's office is an oil painting of César. It appears to the outsider an unremarkable Edwardian portrait of a strong-featured pater-familias, but its prominent presence in the room from which the hotel is directed is not just an act of conventional piety. M. Auzello, essentially a practical man of action, told me suddenly one day that not to have known César Ritz is the greatest regret of his life. 'Very often,' he said, 'when a difficult question arises I turn my eyes towards that portrait and wonder what he would have done in such a case. It has many times helped me to resolve a problem and make the right decision. Even to know *about* him and to have known and worked with people who knew him is enough to give me . . . ' he paused for the English word, '. . . a veneration for César Ritz. I truly feel that even from an oil painting he still supervises the hotel he created.'

Not long ago, in an issue mainly devoted to Paris, *Life* maga-zine—no sycophant when opportunity exists for criticism or even iconoclasm—described the Ritz in one simple, comprehensive, unmodified phrase: 'a great internationally famous hotel which provides luxury with taste'. This could hardly be improved upon as a summary of what César Ritz set out to create. The Ritz is César's living monument, the product of his experience, observa-tion and obsessive thinking on the subject of hotels and restaur-ants in the thirty-odd years from the time when he was a young waiter until 'the little house' in the Place Vendôme opened its doors.

Thus the story of the Ritz is essentially the story of one man, and the circumstances that led to the creation of the hotel that bears his name are as integral as a foundation stone to the story of the hotel itself.

*   *   *

César Ritz was born in the Swiss village of Niederwald in 1850. He was the thirteenth child of a peasant couple, but the family line was long, if humble, and the stone stove in their living-room bore a crest which is still reproduced on the hotel writing paper. His father, Anton, owned a small holding, with a few cows and goats, but he was also mayor of the village, which had a population of under two hundred. There had been painters and altar-carvers in the family and César's mother remarked on her thirteenth child's well-made hands and wondered if he might not become an artist. (This is curious, as Charles Ritz recalls his father bemoaning his 'farmer's hands' and saying, 'What can I do with them?')

The boy went to the local school—a hut to which each child carried a log of wood in winter as his contribution to the heating; in summer he helped to herd his father's beasts. When the boy's further education was discussed, Anton was of the opinion that it was a waste of time. His wife, ambitious for her children, disagreed, but she was not helped by the fact that César himself did not know what he wanted to do. When he was asked if he would like to be an artist, or an engineer, he said he preferred herding the goats. Yet at the same time he wanted to escape from the restricted life of a remote Alpine village. Niederwald lies in a valley, one end closed by the mountains and the other end open. César later said that though he was far from unhappy at home he always gazed longingly at the open end of the valley and dreamed of a life in the great world beyond.

When he was twelve he was sent to Sion, the capital of the canton, to learn French and mathematics. At the end of three years he had not learned much and still had no clear ambition. Anton became impatient. To resolve the matter he paid 300 francs to a friend who owned the Hotel des Trois Couronnes et Poste in the near-by town of Brig, and César became an apprentice wine-waiter.

At the end of a year, M. Escher, the *patron*, said to the boy, 'You will never make anything of yourself in the hotel business. It requires a special flair and I must tell you the truth—you don't have it.'

Too proud to return to Niederwald as a failure, César looked around for a job and found one as an assistant waiter in the local Jesuit seminary. But again he was dismissed. This time it was not for any fault of his own. The sexton of the seminary was always drunk and neglected his work, putting the blame on young César, who at last rebelled. Despising laziness and lying (as he did all his life), he rounded on the sexton and told him he was a good-for-nothing drunkard—and that was the end of that job.

The great Universal Exhibition in Paris in 1867 fired César's imagination. He felt sure there must be jobs for waiters in the crowded capital and off he went. His first job in Paris was at the Hotel de la Fidelité, a small, undistinguished hotel, where he did a little of everything—polishing floors, brushing boots, scrubbing, and running up and down stairs with luggage and trays.

In this period he recorded his first love affair—with a Russian baroness. (When César died he left some notes for a memoir which was never written and Mme Ritz records that he described this initiation in the simple sentence: '*J'eus la chance de devenir l'ami intime d'une charmante baronne russe.*' She also had a photograph of him with the baroness and remarks that he looked 'so elegant, so nonchalant. . . . Even at that early date [there was] little trace if any of his humble peasant background.')

Whether or not the affair of the baroness was the cause, César moved on to a job which was hardly progress; he became a waiter in a workmen's bistro. From this he moved to a restaurant which served lunch for 1fr. 50c. (about 1s. 3d.) but, while he won praise as a willing and speedy waiter, he was fired because of the number of dishes he broke. He had now, however, decided that he wanted to learn the restaurant business thoroughly, and in his next job he worked his way up from assistant waiter to restaurant manager.

Meanwhile, looking around Paris, he fixed his ambitions on Voisin, then the most fashionable restaurant. ('In the lower rooms statesmen and generals discussed affairs of moment over their luncheons . . . poets read unpublished verses to charmed listeners,' Madame Ritz has recorded.) He heard gossip of 'princely romances and amazing supper parties' in the upper rooms. Sarah Bernhardt was a customer and there were South Americans who would spend 100 francs (about £4) dining alone.

[35]

At the very moment when his employer was tempting him with a junior partnership, Ritz resigned. He had been offered a job at Voisin, he said. In fact he had begged a job from Bellenger, the famous proprietor of Voisin. His claims that he spoke several languages, had experience in many aspects of restaurant work, knew wine, and was 'quick, neat and polite', made no impression on Bellenger. But when in desperation he said, 'I am willing to start at the beginning and learn if you will teach me', Bellenger engaged him. The restaurant manager had gone back to being an assistant waiter.

At Voisin, under the severe regime of Bellenger, Ritz learned his job. The waiters were paraded every evening, inspected by Bellenger, reproved for past errors and lectured for the future. Ritz learned to deal with people, to handle eccentrics and celebrities appropriately. Before long customers with famous names were insisting on being served by César.

The celebrities apparently did not always make much impression on the young waiter, except as customers to be satisfied. Years later, when the Goncourt brothers were mentioned in conversation, he said, 'I remember a M. Goncourt. He used to come occasionally to Voisin's . . . a great talker. He wrote plays . . . very depressing plays. I know, for I went to see one. He gave me a free ticket.' But in addition to Mme Bernhardt and M. Goncourt, he served in that period George Sand, Théophile Gautier and the younger Dumas. More important to his career was what he learned from Bellenger. He told his wife later that when Bellenger carved a joint he would make the juices run with the fork—the 'appeal to the eye' which remained one of Ritz's cardinal beliefs about the presentation of food.

Ritz worked devotedly at Voisin, but his stay there did not last very long. He was barely twenty when the Franco-Prussian war began and soon catering de luxe was impossible and catering of any kind extremely difficult. At this time Ritz first heard of a chef named Escoffier. General MacMahon, who came occasionally to Voisin, was more often to be found at the much less celebrated Petit Moulin Rouge, and there he had found the unknown Escoffier, whose praises he sang.

The Siege of Paris lived in the minds of both Ritz and Escoffier, and Mme Ritz recalls hearing them reminisce about the
relative culinary merits of cat, rat, horse and elephant. One of
Voisin's triumphs of the time was to buy two elephants which
were killed in the Paris Zoo. *Elephant trunk, sauce chasseur*
appeared on the menu and 'elephant blood pudding' was generally agreed to be highly enjoyable.

But the days of apprehension and famine had their effect on
Ritz; to the end of his life he could hardly bear to listen to the
Marseillaise because of its associations with 1870. (He was not,
remember, a Frenchman.)

He came to the conclusion that the 'great days' were over,
and Voisin was part of the great days. He wanted a change and
while looking for the right opening he earned a living as a waiter
on the Champs Elysées, descending abruptly from *haute cuisine*
to answering endless calls of '*Garçon—un bock*'.

Now he could not wait to get away from Paris, and at last,
with his Swiss passport, he achieved it. Of this first period in
Paris, Ritz later wrote, 'I had incredible courage and I worked
with ardour because I had great ambition.' And when he left, in a
crowded refugee train, he decided that this was the end of one
world and the beginning of another.

The 'new world'—in two senses—was born for Ritz with the
rich Americans who came to Europe once the war was over.
Morgan, Gould, Vanderbilt, Drexel—such names were to play
a big part in his life, but when he returned to Paris he made a
new start humbly as a floor waiter at the Hotel Splendide. It was
not long before he began to mount the ladder of promotion and in
less than a year he was *maître d'hôtel*. Still in his early twenties,
he became, by what his widow has called 'feats of courage and
diplomacy', not merely a good host and a skilled servant but a
sophisticated guide to the Continent for men with money and
leisure who were sampling Europe for the first time. He is said to
have been the first man who recognised that Americans had to
have ice-water, and supplied it without being asked.

The celebrated 'Commodore' Vanderbilt, founder of the
family fortunes, decided the young Swiss would go a long way

and gave him a piece of advice which Ritz often quoted later—curiously, because it seems neither profound nor necessary in Ritz's case. It was simply, 'Think quick, young man.' He impressed his Splendide employer by habitually thinking quick. The new American clientele were not wine-drinkers by habit, yet it was soon noted that the sales of the best wines from the hotel's cellars were extraordinarily good. The manager asked Ritz if he could explain this profitable phenomenon. There was a Château Lafite 1848, for instance . . .

'I have recommended it,' said Ritz.

The manager pressed a little further. The truth was that Ritz had told his customers that such a wine was the surest antidote to the effects of the dubious local water.

Ritz had now become professionally attached to 'society' and decided that in serving what would now be called the international set his future lay. When the topic of the moment became the International Exhibition to be held in Vienna he decided to go there, even though it meant returning to the level of waiter.

César Ritz was a snob, but only, as it were, functionally; only in so far as snobbery affected his business. With his background, it is not surprising that he was impressed when as a young man he encountered the celebrated and the wealthy, but he never appears to have stood in any awe of them. His decision to cultivate fashionable society, to make an impression on its leaders, was purely a career decision. It was important to have the patronage of the Prince of Wales and he enjoyed it. But he never fawned or failed to speak his mind on professional matters. He never presumed or stepped even fractionally out of line.

He was prepared discreetly to exploit his connections. M. Laurens, the Egyptian cigarette manufacturer, once told Mme Ritz that a great deal of his success was due not so much to the fact that the Prince of Wales smoked his cigarettes as that Ritz put the word around—no more than a murmur at the right moment—that they *were* the Prince's favourites. But always Ritz worked on the simple principle that the hotelier's business was to supply food, wine, accommodation and all the service that these involved, and as he had fastidious and therefore expensive tastes it followed that his clientele was to be found only among people with ample money.

In Vienna he certainly met the famous. The restaurant in which he worked was near the Imperial Pavilion and when the Emperor Franz Josef was entertaining on a large scale the best waiters were borrowed from the restaurant where Ritz worked. It was now that he first served the Prince of Wales and—with Ritz it was automatic—learned his tastes, as his widow put it, 'in food, wine, tobacco, music, women and conversation'. It could never do an ambitious waiter any harm to know how the future King of England liked his beef (well-done) or what cigars he preferred. (In Ritz's case these studies were so well rewarded that in later years the Prince was known to say to him, 'You know better than I do what I like. Arrange a dinner to my taste.')

At these imperial functions in Vienna he served also the German Emperor and his Crown Prince, Bismarck, General Moltke, King Leopold of the Belgians, the Czar and Czarina of Russia, the King of Italy and the princes of Denmark. His Anglophilia was perhaps beginning to form although he had never been to England, for he noted, and deplored, that the German guests were the most honoured and he felt that the Prince of Wales was not accorded the precedence due to him.

When the Vienna Exhibition was over Ritz was doubtful what his next move should be. He was twenty-three, and he felt that time was passing too quickly and he had not yet established himself. Eventually he decided on the South of France and he became restaurant manager of the Grand Hotel, Nice. This was the beginning of what Mme Ritz called his 'wanderings in the wake of a migratory society'.

Switzerland was the fashionable place in summer and Ritz, while in Nice, had caught the eye of Weber, director of the mountain-top hotel at Rigi-Kulm. Before Weber left Nice he had signed Ritz for the coming summer season.

Although difficult of access—provisions, luggage and even guests had to be carried the last part of the journey by horses and mules—Rigi-Kulm was extremely popular. What was curious about its trade was that often, having been crowded in the evening, it would be half-empty by mid-morning. The reason for this was the prevailing fashion for going to Rigi to see the Alpine sunrise.

Half an hour before dawn every morning a cowherd blew his horn and this was the dawn-watchers' reveille. Some were slow to rouse and as the whole point of the excursion was to see the sun rise there were always guests who scrambled out at the last minute in the first clothes they could lay hands on, or even in blankets. Ritz loved to tell, and never failed to laugh himself at, a story of one morning at Rigi when a dignified Victorian Englishman was watching the solar show and a sudden gust of wind whisked away the blanket which was all he was wearing. With a scream of horror he threw himself face down in the snow and would not move until the blanket had been recovered and restored to him.

It was towards the end of his Rigi season that Ritz gave a striking demonstration that he had taken to heart 'Commodore' Vanderbilt's advice to 'think quick'. It was bitterly cold for September and a new central heating system was in operation for the first time. One morning, with the temperature eight degrees below zero, the heating broke down and defied repair. The hotel was almost empty of guests, but suddenly Weber received a telephone message from Cook's in Lucerne that a party of forty Americans on a tour of Europe would be arriving for lunch. They had in fact already left and it was impossible to put them off.

Weber was in despair. Ritz went into action. He called for the day's menu and began to alter it. Weber wailed that this was no time to tinker with menus. What Ritz was ensuring was that the party would at least have hot and heating dishes, beginning with *consommé* and ending with *crêpes flambées*. Then he gave orders for forty bricks to be put in the oven. Next, he summoned the waiters to help him move a table from the restaurant into a smaller drawing-room, decorated in red. (A forty-seater table was not uncommon in those days when *table d'hôte* instead of separate tables was the custom; some of the tables could accommodate a hundred people.) Ritz then gave orders for four large copper bowls, which normally stood in the entrance hall with palms in them, to be moved into the red drawing-room. These were filled with methylated spirit and, when the guests arrived, lit. The room looked far more cheerful than the huge dining-room and with the blazing bowls and a hot brick wrapped in flannel under each guest's feet there were no complaints about the temperature. The luncheon party went off successfully.

It was at Rigi that an incident happened which was to have a decisive influence on Ritz's career. There arrived with one of the dawn parties a distinguished Swiss, Colonel Max Pfyffer, soldier, civil engineer and architect, who had been responsible for many buildings in and around Lucerne, including the Hotel Grand National, which his father-in-law owned. Mme Ritz suggests that Pfyffer had heard of the hot-brick luncheon party, but the essential fact is that Pfyffer, from his own observation, decided that the *maître d'hôtel* was particularly efficient and before leaving he had found out his name and noted it in his diary.

* * *

The idea of having an hotel of his own one day had now taken firm shape in Ritz's mind. But he wanted more experience, and he also wanted to try various kinds of hotel before deciding what he would aim for when he was able to start on his own. He had never worked in a health-resort hotel, but he had heard that there were advantages: the clientele was always moneyed, the seasons were long and the tips were good. He decided he would try such a place and without much difficulty found a job as a *maître d'hôtel* at Locarno, on Lake Maggiore.

Here the young César certainly added to his experience. The manager of the hotel was a hard-drinking man given to such eccentricities as ringing the dinner bell at five o'clock in the morning. Once, when he doubted his wife's fidelity, he chased her through the corridors firing a pistol.

Inevitably the administration of the hotel was erratic; there were double-bookings of rooms, mixed-up luggage and other confusions. Ritz wrote mildly of this experience, 'I did what I could to pacify the clients', but he said later that no job did more to teach him an essential attribute of the good hotelier—diplomacy.

Of the seasonal jobs at which Ritz worked in those years one at least had a lasting effect on him. It was at an hotel at San Remo which was much frequented by tuberculosis sufferers. He had a natural passion for cleanliness, but here, in the presence of disease, he became, as he remained, almost fanatical. It was here he rebelled against the use of heavy furnishing materials—drapes, covers, curtains and fringes which were not easy to take down and were therefore cleaned only at long intervals. It was revolutionary then to decree, as Ritz did, that all fabrics must be washable. Wherever he could he replaced wallpaper with paint. And while he was not able, as manager of a minor hotel, to do much about the shortage of bathrooms he made up his mind that when he had an hotel of his own every bedroom would have its own bathroom. 'Ritz,' said his widow years later, 'was one of the greatest civilising influences of his time as regards hygiene and sanitation.'

At San Remo Colonel Pfyffer came back into Ritz's life, and this time to stay. He was now in control of the National at Lucerne, and he told Ritz that things were not going well. He blamed ignorance and bad management. 'I am not an hotel man,' he said, 'but I have ideas—a gentleman's ideas—of what a great hotel should be. You have imagination and ingenuity. I promise you every facility to carry out your ideas. Perhaps you will make a great career for yourself.' And he offered the astonished Ritz, aged twenty-seven, the managership of the largest and most luxurious hotel in Switzerland.

Despite initial difficulties—a staff become slack through negligent management had to be virtually retrained—Ritz quickly made the National a centre of continental social life; the balls, fêtes, parties and concerts during the July–August season each year were talked about all over Europe.

For eleven years Ritz reigned in summer at Lucerne. In the winters he went to the South of France. One hotel he managed was at Menton, and there he made friends with a family of hoteliers who had, staying with them on a visit, an eleven-year-old schoolgirl relation, Marie-Louise, whom Ritz inevitably met. Nine years later she became Mme Ritz.

One winter Ritz went to Paris and made his first venture as a restaurant owner-manager, renting the buffet of the Jardin d'Acclimatation in the Bois de Boulogne. In Paris he met again the manager for whom he had worked at the Hotel Splendide years before, and who now offered him a partnership in an hotel at Trouville. Ritz discussed the proposition with Colonel Pfyffer. Ritz's attitude was that, as he was now nearly thirty, if he was ever going to fulfil his dream and have his own hotel, this was surely the time to do it. Pfyffer advised against. Monte Carlo was now the fashionable place in winter; with that and summers at Lucerne, what more stable future could Ritz want? But Ritz was restless and impatient. He chose Trouville.

It was at Trouville that Ritz might be said to have graduated in the art of catering exquisitely for the rich. He was up early in the morning marketing; he invented new dishes, often based on very simple local products, and he charged maximum prices. Summer at Trouville became the gourmet's holiday.

But Ritz's perfectionism was expensive. The Trouville season was short and there was not time to recoup his costs and make even a modest profit. He still had to make a living, so when he was offered the position of general manager of the Grand Hotel, Monte Carlo, he accepted, and returned reluctantly to being an employee. But before leaving Trouville he took with him a fine chef he had found and lured away from a private house. With him he made a success of the Grand, even in face of the competition of the new and sumptuous Hotel de Paris. The famous went out of their way to visit the Grand. When Queen Victoria was staying at Menton she drove over to Monte Carlo several times, accompanied by her famous Scots retainer, John Brown, to lunch or dine at Ritz's hotel.

Then the inevitable happened; the powerful rival, the Hotel de Paris, lured away his chef. But Ritz was less upset by this than might be expected. The chef had often talked to Ritz about the man who had taught him all he knew. Ritz had heard the name before—Auguste Escoffier. Ritz sent for him and as Mme

Ritz says, 'the association of Ritz and Escoffier was one of the most fortunate things that ever happened in either of the two men's lives'. Together they evolved their ideas of what a de luxe hotel should be, in comfort, cuisine and service.

They found that they were in agreement on items of their hotel credo which were not generally held, for instance that food and its presentation should be aimed primarily at the women guests. Escoffier was not only a great chef; he was an organiser, and his kitchens were run meticulously. The chaos which often reigned even in kitchens from which good food emerged had long been a source of despair to Ritz. Escoffier cared about order and cleanliness as much as Ritz did. He cared too about what happened to the food after it left his kitchen. Like Ritz, he believed that even the best food is the better for being really hot and the best meals enhanced by the quality of the china and glass on the table.

Meanwhile Marie-Louise had finished her education and was learning the family business of hotel-keeping in Monte Carlo. She learned quickly and enthusiastically, but in her free time 'there were many opportunities to meet and cultivate the friendship of the new manager of the Grand Hotel'. They had a great deal in common and became close friends. Ritz claimed that he soon made up his mind she was the girl he wanted to marry, but he waited until she was of marrying age and until he felt that he was a man of substance.

In 1887 he decided the time had come. He gave up his connections with Monte Carlo and Lucerne and, in the face of stiff local competition, took over the Restaurant de la Conversation in Baden-Baden. At the same time, raising the last penny he could, he acquired the Hotel de Provence in Cannes. Then he married. He was thirty-seven and Marie-Louis was twenty.

Ritz also acquired a small hotel at Baden-Baden, the Minerva. The restaurant there became a meeting-place for international society and soon he had put the Provence on the social map as well; the clinching success came when the Prince of Wales decided to stay there for an Easter holiday. Thereafter he came every season.

A particularly lavish party Ritz organised for a German prince, transforming the Restaurant de la Conversation into a woodland scene, attracted the attention of an Englishman, Rupert D'Oyly Carte, who was in Baden taking the cure. 'This,' said D'Oyly Carte, 'is the sort of thing I would like in my new hotel in London.' He was at that time building the hotel of his dreams—the Savoy—and tried to tempt Ritz to join him.

But Ritz was very happy in his freedom, running and perfecting his two small hotels. Soon afterwards, however, Ritz received another proposal from D'Oyly Carte: that he should go to London for the opening of the Savoy and make a few suggestions. It was D'Oyly Carte's idea that he could gain, especially in attracting the right clientele, by giving the impression that Ritz was somehow connected with the Savoy. As the payment proposed was the equivalent of D'Oyly Carte's own year's earnings as chairman of the hotel, Ritz accepted.

*   *   *

This first period at the Savoy convinced Ritz that the social capital of the world and the ideal place for a luxury hotel was London. But he was doubtful if the Savoy was right; the cuisine, for instance, he found uninteresting. Six months later the Savoy management decided that things were not satisfactory and asked Ritz to take over the management on his own terms.

Within a few months Ritz, accompanied by his friend and *chef de cuisine*, Escoffier, had conquered London. Otto Kahn, the banker, proclaimed that Ritz was a great man because he had made London, at last, 'a place worth living in'. Coquelin, the actor, complimented Ritz on having revolutionised hotels and the habits of society, but challenged him to do something about the English laws which prevented restaurants being open after 11 p.m. or on Sundays. Ritz accepted the challenge and applied all his characteristic determination to campaigning for this reform. He 'lobbied' such Savoy customers as Henry Labouchere, journalist and M.P., Mrs Langtry and Lord Randolph Churchill; he talked his own board of directors (who were pessimistic) into working on people of influence they knew.

He succeeded. Legislation was passed and the Savoy's restaurant was open till half past midnight, and Sunday dinner was not only served but became a feature of the week. 'A revolution was thus effected in London's life,' Mme Ritz wrote. As English bakers don't work on Saturdays, and Ritz wanted fresh bread on Sunday, he sent to Vienna for a baker, with the result that crusty Viennese rolls became part of all Ritz's service. He also introduced orchestras at dinner (starting with Johann Strauss) because he noticed that in England, unlike the Continent, silence was apt to fall upon diners and he was sure this tended to make them go home earlier than they would otherwise. With music they lingered over dinner and the increase in wine takings more than paid for the orchestra.

Ritz was now in a position to lay down the law and set precisely the tone he desired. He made evening dress compulsory in the dining-rooms and banned ladies wearing hats or unaccompanied by gentlemen. When a celebrated courtesan complimented Ritz and said, 'You have reached the height of your profession—as I have in mine', César permitted himself one of his rare witticisms addressed to a customer. 'Alas,' he said, 'with far less pleasure and far more trouble than you have experienced, mademoiselle.'

*   *   *

In this Savoy period, Ritz was in his forties and at the peak of his prodigious powers. His success at the Savoy was such, in terms of his impact on the social life of London, that he was seriously accused of breaking up home life. 'Dining out' became a growing habit and the Savoy was the most fashionable rendezvous. Ritz also had an effect on London club life; men who would previously have dined at their men-only clubs now took their wives out to dinner or supper at the Savoy.

Although it affected only the small upper layer known as 'society', this was a real social revolution. André L. Simon describes it thus: 'There had been up to that time two very different sorts of "smart" women in London, Paris, New York and other great cities: those whose heart's desire—and profession or vocation—was to please men; and the others: they did not mix. It was only in the late eighties, with César Ritz at the Savoy . . . that a new and much higher standard of elegance was introduced into the catering world: for the first time *grand luxe* and *bon goût* were happily partnered, and for the first time also the wives, sisters and daughters of members of the old aristocracy and of captains of industry and of wealthy financiers dined with their male escorts in fashionable public places, where they had no objection whatever—far from it—to meeting all the more glamorous cocottes of the day.'*

Yet Ritz's activities were by no means confined to one hotel. His connections and plans were steadily expanding. When he took over the direction of the Savoy he was also responsible for the Hotel de Provence in Cannes and the Hotel Minerva and the Restaurant de la Conversation at Baden-Baden. In the course of this decade he was actively engaged in hotel enterprises in Rome, Frankfurt, Salsomaggiore, Palermo, Biarritz, Wiesbaden, Monte Carlo, Lucerne and Menton and was involved in projects for hotels in Cairo, Madrid and Johannesburg. By the end of the decade, by which time the Ritz in Paris was open, he had withdrawn from all of these but had acquired controlling interests in nine other restaurants and hotels, the principal of which, apart from the Paris Ritz, was the Carlton in London.

'It is difficult to untangle the confusing and multitudinous events of those years,' Mme Ritz wrote later. 'How quickly things moved then! How energetic we were! How filled were the days; each hour squeezed of its last second's value. Life was indeed exciting . . . César's suitcases were never completely unpacked; he was always either just arriving from or departing upon some new journey. Every year brought its new project, every month some new crisis, disappointment, struggle, or triumph. Until 1893 the itinerary he followed lay chiefly between London, Cannes, and Baden-Baden; then for three years between London, Aix-les-Bains, and Rome; then Frankfurt-am-Main, Lucerne, Monte Carlo, and Biarritz; then London, Salsomaggiore, and Paris.'

It was in this mobile period that the infant Charles Ritz

* *The History of Champagne* (Ebury Press, 1962).

[47]

became what he described as 'a connoisseur of luggage racks', having been so often made to sleep in them.

In addition to his travels, Ritz's correspondence at this time was enormous. There were directives to be issued in connection with his far-flung plans, but he never forgot day-to-day details. His letters to the men on the spot were peppered with instructions concerning individual guests—who had dry toast for breakfast or cherry jam for tea; which brand of whisky one man drank and which mineral water another must have by his bed; Mr X who was very tall insisted on an eight-foot bed; Lady Y had to be called at 7.30 a.m. *precisely*.

It was little wonder that Ritz's doctor said to him, 'Take it easy, you're killing yourself.' But Ritz did not know how to rest.

The aeroplane would, of course, have simplified Ritz's travelling problems, but even though earthbound he achieved some feats of travel expertise remarkable for that time. He devised, for example, a method of getting from Paris to London by which he lost only a fraction of a working day and did not miss a night's sleep in his own bed. By leaving Paris about four in the afternoon he could pick up the Basle Express at Amiens, have dinner on the train, and be in London before midnight.

Yet miraculously the Ritzes continued to have a home life. They first bought a house in Hampstead, where their second and last child, René, was born. Then they moved to a large, rambling house with a big garden in what was then 'the country'—now the closely-built suburb of Golders Green. In summer Ritz moved out of his Savoy apartment and spent as much time as possible at Golders Green. He rode in the morning with a doctor friend. He and Mme Ritz followed the social custom of walking or driving in Hyde Park.

They entertained at Golders Green at the week-ends and it was there in 1897 that, in a few minutes, a small but permanent addition was made to the dinner tables of the world. The Ritzes were having tea on the lawn one Sunday with Escoffier when Mme Ritz complained that toast was never thin enough for her. Ritz and Escoffier discussed this and Ritz suggested toasting a slice of bread, cutting it through and toasting it again. Escoffier disappeared into the house and re-emerged with 'a plateful of thin, crisp, curling wafers'. 'A new dish,' he said triumphantly, 'and it's called Toast Marie'—after Mme Ritz. She thought this was not distinctive enough as a name and when soon afterwards Dame Nellie Melba, back from an American tour, came to the Savoy and announced that she was on a diet in which dry toast played a large part, Ritz introduced the 'new dish' and announced that henceforth it would be known as Toast Melba.

Among the clientele of the Savoy there was one who while appreciating most of what Ritz had to offer was opposed to 'modern improvements'. This pocket of reaction was Oscar Wilde. Almost any innovation Ritz made, outside the culinary realm, Wilde rejected. 'Who wants an immovable washing basin in one's room?' he said. 'I do not. Hide the thing. I prefer to ring for water when I need it.' Electric light, he complained, was everywhere except where you need it—'a harsh and ugly light, enough to ruin your eyes, and not a candle or a lamp for bedside reading.' Wilde didn't even like elevators. They went too fast for him.

It was during Ritz's Savoy period that his original sponsor, Colonel Pfyffer, died. His two sons, Hans and Alphonse, friends and admirers of Ritz, were both in the hotel business. Hans now took over control of the National at Lucerne and Alphonse was managing the Grand in Rome. He interested Ritz in the possibilities of making this one of the great luxury hotels of the world and together they rebuilt and transformed it. The months he spent on this task were César's introduction to Rome. He loved it and for a time even thought of making it his headquarters. When he entered St Peter's for the first time he stopped at the doorway, enraptured by its size and splendour. Then he exclaimed, 'What a magnificent banquet room this would make!'

But once the new Grand was successfully launched Ritz again found the natural hub of his scattered empire in London. For him, the way of life of the society which centred on the Prince of Wales and the 'Marlborough House set' was the most elegant and sophisticated—though far from representative of the Victorian England in which it flourished—and all his life

[49]

his criteria were those of 'the English gentry'. Indeed, in a sense Ritz never left London. As soon as his Paris hotel was a *fait accompli* he turned his energies to making of the Carlton 'another Ritz'—and it was there his first collapse came. But that is to anticipate the quite unforeseeable circumstances which provided the impetus for the Paris venture which was to be the centrepiece and masterwork of his career.

CHAPTER THREE

THE DREAM REALISED

FOR ALL the multiplicity of César Ritz's hotel interests in the Nineties there was still one thing missing, one dream unfulfilled. No Ritz Hotel yet existed. It seems clear that he was biding his time until he could find the right place and the right circumstances in which to create what had gradually built up in his mind as the perfect hotel. It would not be large but it would embody all he had learned from his varied experience and all the theories he had not yet had a chance to put into practice.

He had made many friends in London and some of them not merely appreciated his talents but were ready to invest in any new enterprise he might wish to tackle.

Prominent among these was a group of influential men in the City of London who made the Savoy their social headquarters. These were men who had made and were making fortunes out of the gold and diamond mines of South Africa. Their business affairs took them often to Paris and they complained that they could not find an hotel entirely to their taste. Shortage of bathrooms was one of the principal faults they found. This was a lack in Paris of which Ritz was well aware. Although his dream of the perfect hotel was not necessarily identified with Paris, he had never forgotten a tiny incident which happened there.

One day, walking through the Place Vendôme, he saw a horse-drawn cart outside an hotel. A copper bathtub and two big containers of water were being unloaded. Ritz asked the carters what was going on and was told that, in effect, a hot bath was being delivered for the Prince of Wales. The whole procedure seemed to Ritz so cumbersome and primitive that he reavowed his promise to himself that one day, when he had his own hotel, there would be a bathroom for every room.

Now his moneyed City friends were urging Ritz to make an hotel in Paris—with their financial backing.

One of those friends was a lawyer, Henry V. Higgins, a colourful character who had started his career in the Life Guards, but turned to the law when he lost so much money gambling on horse-racing that he had to resign his commission. He prospered and became an important figure in society, described as London's most fashionable solicitor. Two of his associates, who became Ritz's first backers, were Leopold Hirsch and the Baron Jacques de Gunzbourg.

Ritz, who had no French blood in his veins and who had never worked in Paris above the rank of restaurant manager, responded to their suggestion, but he did not jump at it. The idea attracted him, but, he pointed out, it would be very difficult to find the right place, as he had definite ideas about the hotel in Paris or anywhere else on which he would be prepared to stake his name and reputation.

In 1896, however, a company, the Ritz Hotel Syndicate Ltd, was registered in London and the original subscribers, in addition to Ritz and Higgins, were Ritz's personal team at the Savoy— Escoffier, the chef, Echenard, the *maître d'hôtel*, Agostini, the cashier, Baumgartner, the staff manager, and Collins, Ritz's private secretary.

Accounts vary as to how the Place Vendôme location was chosen. The incident of the Prince of Wales's bath, Charles Ritz thinks, predisposed his father in favour of the locality. Joseph Duveen, the art dealer (later Lord Duveen), is said to have been responsible for discovering that the house at No. 15, then occupied by the Crédit Mobilier bank, was about to come on the market and urged it upon Ritz as the place for a de luxe hotel. (Certainly Duveen was always a lover of the Place Vendôme. He leased the space occupied by the stables in the courtyard of No. 20 and in 1907 built there a beautiful pavilion modelled on the Petit Trianon, which became his favourite house of business.)

But another version has it that when Ritz, Pfyffer and de Gunzbourg went to Paris to look for a site for a Ritz Hotel, César favoured one at the Trocadero—with his Swiss origin, it has been suggested to me, he was naturally attracted by hills—while Pfyffer's preference as a business man was for a site where the Olympia music hall now stands in the Boulevard des Capucines, a few minutes' walk from the Ritz. This was then a horse-bus depot and would have been the cheapest site as well as being in the busiest district. De Gunzbourg, the only Parisian of the three, voted for the Place Vendôme, although at that time it was in a run-down, neglected state, with grass growing up between the paving stones.

Whatever the precise truth of this, there is no doubt that the decision of the Crédit Mobilier to move from what had been the town house of the Duc de Lauzun (who led the French cavalry at Yorktown in 1781) gave the hotel men an opportunity too good to be missed.

Speed was essential if the property was not to slip through their fingers and a large sum was being asked for even an eight-day option. Ritz, who always moved quickly, decided to anticipate his backers' decision. He remembered from years earlier a man who had said he would be under a debt of gratitude to him all his life. This was Marnier Lapostolle, a wealthy owner of vineyards who had once brought to Ritz a liqueur he had invented. Ritz tasted it and approved. Lapostolle decided to put it on the market, but he needed a name for it. Lapostolle was a little man, inclined to pomposity. Ritz said, half ironically, 'Why not call it "Le Grand Marnier"?' Lapostolle did, and made a fortune from Grand Marnier, still one of the most popular of liqueurs. Lapostolle readily put up the money Ritz asked for and the option was secured.

The house at No. 15 suited Ritz in every way. He wanted his hotel to be small, intimate and exclusive. He had no wish to disturb the elegant Mansard façade and, though he did not know how, he was determined to recreate the interior with 'all the refinements of living that a prince might hope to incorporate in his town house'.

But he had difficulty in communicating his enthusiasm to his financial backers, eager as they were to see a Ritz Hotel launched. They thought the house too small to be profitable. They had visualised something on a much larger scale. They were horrified that Ritz did not even intend to build over the gardens; indeed he insisted that his hotel must have gardens. But Ritz was adamant and backed his confidence with an offer to guarantee them a six per cent return on their money in the first year, which he fulfilled.

The backers decided to swallow their misgivings and go along with Ritz, so the first object of the Ritz Hotel Syndicate Ltd was formally described as being to acquire 'a piece of land in the Place Vendôme in the City of Paris and the Republic of France together with all buildings erected thereon, and to complete, alter, increase and develop the said buildings and property when acquired as an hotel with all the usual and desirable adjuncts and conveniences'.

The company did not, of course, confine itself to this and the objects as set forth in the original Articles of Association also entitled the company 'to purchase lease or acquire other property or hotels anywhere; to carry on the business of hotel, restaurant, tavern and lodging-house keepers, licensed victuallers, wine, beer and spirit merchants, importers and dealers in food and foreign and colonial produce of all descriptions, hairdressers, perfumers, job-masters, livery stable keepers, proprietors of baths and laundries, tobacco and cigar merchants, agents for railway companies and carriers, theatrical and opera box-office proprietors and general agents and any other business or businesses which may be, or may be deemed by the Directors to be, of a nature calculated to assist or promote the Company's business'.

Further objects included, for reasons now obscure, 'to construct, control or manage' water-works, reservoirs, tramways and places of worship as well as hotels, restaurants, clubs and casinos;

to carry on business as dealers in sand and lime and to lend money with or without security.

Almost all Ritz's initial capital was English (the Armenian oil magnate, Calouste Gulbenkian, was in from the start) and the original board of directors consisted of—in addition to Henry Higgins as chairman and Ritz himself as managing director—the Hon. A. G. Brand, M.P., Earl de Grey (a close friend of the Prince of Wales) and the Marquis d'Hautpoul, who had made his home in England and whose English wife was a lady-in-waiting to Queen Alexandra.

Ritz remained at the Savoy for another year, however, and his departure—an unforeseeable event which precipitated his concentration on the Paris Ritz—involved an unlikely and purely personal drama, one of the few battles of will Ritz was ever known to lose.

Mrs W. (Mme Ritz never revealed her identity further) was a housekeeper at the Savoy when Ritz arrived. It was soon apparent that she did not like him or his methods and she opposed and obstructed him in every way she could. The trouble began early when Ritz was reorganising the Savoy staff. Ritz had no use for anybody who would not fall in line with his methods and when Mrs W. proved obdurate Ritz felt he had no other course than to discharge her. But this was not so easy. Mrs W. had influence; she was a close friend of one of the directors and Ritz found it impossible to dislodge her.

The more Ritz made a success of the hotel the more implacable became Mrs W.'s hostility. Eventually, after Ritz had endured years of 'interference, criticism, intrigue, complaints and quarrels' the issue came to a head. Mrs W. demanded that 'rights' of which she alleged Ritz had deprived her should be restored and she presented an ultimatum to her director friend. Ritz's reaction was in effect 'Either that woman goes or I do'—and it was Ritz who went.

He was sufficiently upset by this to offer his resignation to the directors of his own company, but they responded with a vote of confidence. Escoffier, Echenard, Agostini and Henry Elles, the restaurant manager, all resigned from the Savoy immediately, despite Ritz's urging that they should stay at least until they had other jobs to go to. When Ritz told his fellow directors of this the company decided to pay all the salaries as from that date and to regard this devoted group as the nucleus of the new Paris Ritz staff.

This helped to restore Ritz's spirits and other things completed the process. The manager of the Charing Cross Hotel immediately gave the Ritzes his best available apartment; leaders of London society, from the Duchess of Devonshire to Mrs Langtry and Melba, hastened to reassure them with messages and bouquets, and Lady de Grey called specially to convey the news that the Prince of Wales, when he heard what had happened, cancelled a party he had arranged at the Savoy and said, 'Where Ritz goes I go'.

*   *   *

For the next two years all Ritz's fanatical energy was devoted to the creation, with every detail exactly right, of what he later described as the 'little house to which I am very proud to see my name attached'.

Ritz had great taste but he also had humility; he would never pretend knowledge where he did not possess it. When he started to plan the transformation of No. 15 Place Vendôme he said to his wife, 'I have no knowledge of architecture and little of decoration. I know what I need for perfect efficiency and elegance in the hotel I want but I haven't the least idea how to create it.' He said later that his lucky star must have guided him to the architect Charles Mewes. The two men complemented each other perfectly. Mewes shuddered when Ritz said that his hotel must be the 'most modern' in Paris. In 1897 an architect of taste did not respond happily to the word 'modern'. But Mewes soon realised that what Ritz wanted was to avoid elaboration and artificiality, then all too common. Ritz further defined his requirements as 'hygienic, efficient, and beautiful'. Mewes made the understanding between them complete by saying that the beauty must be of a sort that would last for ever—and Ritz agreed.

Experience and observation had given Ritz a number of firm convictions about hotels. One was the handling of light. Electric lighting was new but it had clearly come to stay and Ritz saw that it could be adapted to aesthetic ends; instead of being merely bright and glaring it could be used to show, for instance, women's clothes, jewellery and complexions to good, and even flattering, advantage. 'For weeks,' says Mme Ritz, 'Ritz was absorbed in lighting problems. For hours at a time I would sit while he and an electrician tried the effects of various colour shades on my complexion.' He decided that a delicate apricot pink was the most becoming colour. The shading and placing of lights in restaurants is now commonplace, but Ritz was well ahead of his time—a time when, as Mme Ritz says, 'the last word in artistic lighting was considered to be a bronze nymph holding up a cluster of naked light-bulbs in lieu of flowers'.

Ritz was also a pioneer of indirect lighting. For his main dining-room he chose alabaster urns which threw their light upwards on to a tinted ceiling. In the bedrooms the bowls were suspended from the ceiling by silk cords. The importance of lighting has continued to be a subject of careful study at the Ritz and when only a few years ago the new grill-room was being planned Charles Ritz took great pains to have table lights evolved which would amply light the plate while giving the room in general an almost dim light in keeping with the modern taste for an 'intimate' atmosphere.

His experience at the sanatorium hotel at San Remo had, as I have said, intensified Ritz's obsession for cleanliness, his dislike of the fashionable heavy fabrics—plushes and velvets were the favourites—which collected dust and were not easily cleanable or washable. He preferred paint to wallpaper for the same reason and he would not have wooden beds, as metal was more hygienic. Counterpanes had to be light in weight and colour so that they could be often and easily washed. He even introduced chamois skin sheets under the linen sheets for extra cleanliness.

He rebelled against what was the central feature of most big hotels—a large and luxurious lobby. He thought this encouraged people from outside—'loiterers', he said, who had nothing to do with the hotel. Hence the absence in the Ritz to this day of a 'lounge'.

Wherever possible Ritz installed built-in wardrobes and cup-boards. (One of the abiding joys of the Ritz, in these space-pinching days of hotel design, is that the hanging accommodation is abundant, even extravagant.) He meticulously designed the interiors of his fitted cupboards and closets. He consulted his wife on the blueprints, asking how much hanging space, how many shelves, how many drawers 'an average woman' would require. His 'average woman' was, of course, a lady of wealth and fashion. Mme Ritz pointed out that there was no special drawer for false hair: a deep drawer to hold artificial 'buns, rolls and rats', she said, was essential. Mewes, Mme Ritz recalls, smiled tolerantly, but her husband took the point with typical seriousness and the design was altered to include an additional drawer of the right dimensions.

In March 1898, three months before the date of the opening, the Ritzes moved into one of the top-floor apartments. From there they supervised the completion of the work. Each night when the workmen had gone César and Marie-Louise would walk through the rooms noting what had been done in the day and planning for the next. Ritz made elaborate notes—a new lamp needed here, a wall that was too bare must have a tapestry, a room with a fine view must have thinner net curtains, a room with a north light was too cold and the pale blue curtains must be lined with pale rose, a drawer did not slide in and out smoothly enough, a lock was imperfect; and next morning his first task was to see that each point was put right. He personally instructed housekeepers and maids in bedmaking. Sometimes when a bed looked perfect even to Mme Ritz, he would say there was something wrong and when it was turned down a cover or sheet would be found to have a wrinkle in it, or a pillow had not been plumped up correctly.

*   *   *

Two weeks before the opening night the tables and chairs for the dining-room had not been delivered. Ritz's own fastidiousness had met its match in the cabinet-maker he had chosen; he was a craftsman who would not be hurried. Even with all Ritz's urging and pleading it was not until within a week of the opening that the furniture arrived. They all gathered to admire. Colonel Hans Pfyffer sat down on one of the rose-brocade-covered chairs and declared it comfortable as well as beautiful. 'But,' he added, 'it is a pity you didn't have at least half of them made as arm-chairs. There is nothing like a really comfortable chair to keep people long at the table.' Ritz took the point immediately and several dozen chairs were rushed back to the maker to have arms put on them. Mewes had to do a rush job drawing the design for the arms.

The chairs did not arrive back until the morning of the opening and were quickly put into place. Ritz tried one and Mme Ritz saw his face cloud over. 'The tables are too high,' he said. 'They must go back and be cut down.' Mewes tried a chair and agreed. Ritz dashed out in time to see the van which had delivered the chairs drawing away. He ran after it in the rain and gave his instructions. 'Two centimetres off every table leg and they must be back in two hours.' 'Impossible,' he was told. Couldn't he use them for the opening and have the work done later? Ritz was adamant. Nothing was impossible. In the end the tables came back and the waiters were finishing laying them as the first guests' carriages arrived.

It was still raining. This was another worry for Ritz. Would the invited guests come? The rain stopped, but even then Ritz was still unhappy that his gardens did not look their best. But the guests came—'tout Paris'.

Ritz had said he wanted his hotel to have the atmosphere of a private house, and for all the formality of the opening it was, just under the surface, a domestic scene too: Ritz concealing all his worries and nervousness—'calm and smiling, elegant in his black redingote', his wife wrote—greeting his guests in the lobby, characteristically never faltering on a name, while at the top of the stairway, peering down anxiously, was Mme Ritz with Charles, aged eight, and the toddler René, clinging to her skirts.

The opening was a total success; Mme Ritz's account of it is a glittering list of the socially important names of the period, though now it would be impossible in many cases to explain who they were or, apart from their titles, why they were important:

Boni and Anna de Castellane, Comtesse de Pourtales, Princess Lucien Murat, Marquis du Bourg de Bozas, Vicomtesse Leon de Janze, Comtesse de Salverte, Mme de Levis-Mirepoix, Marquis de Ganay, Comtesse de Chevigné, the Duc and Duchesse d'Uzès, the Duc and Duchesse de Rohan, the Duc and Duchesse de Morny, Pierre de Fouquières, Anthony Drexel ('that Beau Brummell of the American colony'), the Grand Dukes Michael and Alexander, Mrs William Corey, Santos Dumont, Saturno di Unzue, Souza Dantas, the Cobos, the Santa Marias, Marquis de Villalobar, Izzet Bey, Paris Singer, the Goulds, the Vanderbilts and 'the most celebrated beauties of the day—Liane de Pougy, Emilienne d'Alençon, the beautiful Otero. . . .'*

From England came the Dukes of Marlborough, Portland, Sutherland and Norfolk, with their duchesses.

And suddenly, in the midst of the sonorous roll-call one sentence of Mme Ritz's still comes fascinatingly alive: 'Marcel Proust was there, small, dark and nervous-looking, effacing himself behind some person considered to be more important.'

The idea of dining out was still an amusing novelty. The celebrated Boni de Castellane brought his aunt, Princesse Antoine Radziwill, to dinner at the Ritz and he later told César that she had been reluctant to come, but that when she returned home she wrote to him, 'I did think it so amusing when you took me to dine at the inn'.

It was Castellane who on the opening night paid Ritz the compliment he always remembered. As he was leaving he said, 'I am going to dismiss my chef. It is foolish to try to compete with you and Escoffier.'

*　　　*　　　*

* These last three were the most famous courtesans of the day—'the three top members of this brazenly spectacular coterie . . . known as "Les Grandes Trois",' as Cornelia Otis Skinner calls them in her book *Elegant Wits and Grand Horizontals* (Michael Joseph, 1963).

With the Ritz successfully launched César, while keeping the closest watch on its operations, contrived to give much of his attention to the Carlton in London, in which he and his backers had acquired a controlling interest. The one operation was in a sense an extension of the other; all that Ritz and his architect Mewes had learned from their experience in Paris they applied to the rebuilding of the Carlton—more wardrobe and cupboard space, bigger and better private bathrooms; the Carlton was the first London hotel to have a bath to every room.

In the underground grill-room Ritz overcame the sense of being in a basement by putting in double panes of frosted glass with lights between. There was no place for a garden, so he decided to make a feature of the Palm Court and to give it a glass roof. Here, in spite of his backers' protests about extravagances, he moved the dining-room wall back a couple of yards to give the Palm Court a balcony. When asked why, he said it was because the Prince of Wales would appreciate a private corner of the Palm Court. 'How often do you think the Prince of Wales will dine here?', he was asked sceptically. 'Very frequently,' said Ritz confidently.

He counted on patronage from the Marlborough House set, his Savoy clientele and the leading figures of the theatre and opera—the latter because Harry Higgins and Lady de Grey were on the governing board of Covent Garden. The Carlton opened a year after the Paris Ritz and was an immediate success, paying a seven per cent dividend in its first year. The success inspired the idea of a London Ritz and the Piccadilly-Green Park site was bought and work begun.

When Queen Victoria died two years later Ritz realised that his most important customer, the Prince of Wales, would no longer have the same freedom to dine out and give parties in hotels. But he felt sure the Edwardian court would be gay and social life lively. To begin with there would be Edward's coronation and Ritz determined that so far as possible the Carlton would be the centre of London society's celebrations. 'Great days ahead,' he said.

The date of the coronation was announced—26 June 1902.

The Carlton was booked out long in advance and every table for the gala dinner reserved. The windows of the Carlton would be an ideal place from which to watch the procession as it passed along Pall Mall. It was a hot summer and Ritz, up to the eyes in preparations for the festivities, occasionally complained of fatigue. One day he returned home early to Golders Green, exhausted. 'I'm not ill,' he told his wife, 'only tired. When this is all over I'll take a long rest.' Mme Ritz recalled him sitting in a garden chair with his eyes shut, and saying, 'We might as well face it—I am an old man now.' He was not yet fifty-two.

Two days before the coronation the King was taken ill. It was announced that an immediate operation for perityphlitis* was necessary and the coronation was indefinitely postponed. Ritz, his colleagues recalled later, took the news with remarkable calm, issuing the necessary orders to unwind the elaborate arrangements already so far advanced. But suddenly during the afternoon he fainted. When he came round he claimed to be all right but agreed to go home. He had to be helped into the house by his coachman, and Mme Ritz called a doctor. Ritz was put to bed with sedatives but he became delirious. The doctor's verdict was a complete nervous breakdown. Mme Ritz asked how long until he might hope to be well again. 'Maybe a few months,' said the doctor, 'maybe a year, maybe longer . . .'

In the sixteen years between his collapse and his death César Ritz never again resumed the role that was his life—hotelier extraordinary, absorbed and dynamic, living and thinking hotels every waking hour. There seems no doubt that a generation later this malady which struck him down would have been curable, but at the time the only prescription was rest.

No doctor's orders could have been less agreeable to Ritz. Idleness was anathema to him; the whole idea of a long rest was totally against the grain of his character. At first he obeyed his doctor's orders so far as he was able; he stayed away from his hotels for the first time in his life; that he made a sincere effort to obey is obvious from a touching phrase he used in a letter to a

* An intestinal condition originating in the appendix. A few years later it would have been called appendicitis.

friend: 'I have had to learn to do nothing.' But he firmly believed that before long he would be back to normal and whenever his health permitted he busied himself with a thousand details and a mass of plans.

There is extant a journal containing handwritten copies of his correspondence between late November 1903 and early February 1904 when he was living in a villa near Cannes. In that brief period he wrote 394 letters. Even on Christmas Day he is writing to London, hoping that 'the difficulties with the neighbours of the new hotel' (the Ritz) will soon 'arrange themselves'; apparently the trouble was over the height of the building and Ritz was anxious that they would not have to sacrifice too much of the upper floors. On Boxing Day alone he wrote nine letters on a wide variety of subjects.

The letters are consistently optimistic and totally devoid of self-pity. He never complains of anything more specific than occasional fatigue and an attack of *la grippe*. He writes confidently of 'a speedy return to full activity'; by the spring he 'will start working again both in Paris and London'. Repeated again and again in his letters are phrases like 'I am quite myself again' and 'I am very well and ready to discuss any business.' He asks for arrangements to be made for him to inspect examples of furniture—'Louis XIV, Louis XV, Louis XVI, Empire and Sheridan' [Sheraton?] when he comes to London in the spring.

On hotel matters he shows all his old acuity, although one cannot but be touched by the time devoted by the sick man to trivial matters which he should, and could easily, have delegated. He is anxious to boost his health-resort hotel at Salsomaggiore and writes personally to inquirers, enclosing brochures and quoting prices. He takes trouble over testimonials for former employees; he writes to a young man in Ilkley, Yorkshire, at considerable length telling him that while there is no vacancy for a clerk at the Ritz ('it is a small house, with restricted staff') he should try Salsomaggiore for a seasonal job. He explains to Charles's schoolmaster that the boy will be two or three days late in returning to school as he has had bronchitis. He writes to the Mayor of Cannes about the clearing away of garbage, to the post office when his telephone goes wrong; he even remembers to send a doctor's certificate to the London licensing authorities when his licence to sell wine from 4a Cockspur Street (the Ritz Development Company office) is due for renewal and he cannot apply in person. He is patient and polite with a tiresome Income Tax official who keeps writing direct to him although referred several times to his London accountant. He writes to the London tax authorities also to point out that they have failed to give him an allowance for the premiums he pays for life insurance. He writes to claim a refund on an unused first-class railway ticket from Ventimiglia to Paris. He asks for the *Financial News* and the *Financial Times* to be sent to him twice a week. He advises a friend who is suffering from insomnia to take a hot bath at night and make 'moderate use' of sulphonal tablets.

He writes mostly in French but often in excellent English, and occasionally in a mixture—as to his old backer, Mr Higgins, who has had an accident. He hopes '*vous êtes maintenant* all right again.'

One letter in the book is written by Madame Ritz. She asks M. Elles, the manager in Paris, to ensure that the *New York Herald* and other papers will publish an item that 'the main personality of the Christmas celebrations, M. Ritz, will not be present, but several of his friends have stated that he is almost completely well again'.

César obviously hates missing the Christmas Eve gala and writes suggesting people who should be invited; he wants to know immediately afterwards how the evening went.

When Elles reports a particularly glittering array of celebrities dining at the Ritz, César replies at once with instructions that this should be publicised in *Le Figaro* 'with details of the menus, as this makes good publicity, costs nothing and has much effect in the provinces and abroad'.

When, at New Year, he is told that the Czar of Russia has praised a chicken dish, he 'hopes the whole Russian colony has been informed of the Czar's appreciation'.

Discreet publicity occupies M. Ritz a good deal. He asks a Mr Graham, of Bedford Street, London, how many paragraphs and articles he will write about Salsomaggiore for twenty guineas. Apparently Mr Graham suggested that he should be paid by results, for a little later César is agreeing to this but adding that when Mr Graham sends his account it must be accompanied by *all the cuttings.*

He consults the manager of Shepheard's Hotel, Cairo, as to the best Egyptian papers to advertise in, as there have been some Egyptians at Salsomaggiore and this is valuable custom to attract, because they come at exactly the season when they are most needed. He arranges, with the help of an acquaintance in London who has knowledge of South Africa, to advertise in the brochures of the Union Castle steamships and in South African newspapers. He offers the *Home Journal* of Boston photographs to illustrate an article they are going to publish on Salsomaggiore.

He tells London to publicise 'in all the papers where it will do good' the fact that the Queen of Sweden has been staying at his hotel in Frankfurt—but to time the announcement for immediately after the Queen has left. He believes such items often appear as news 'fillers' at the bottom of columns, but, if necessary, a paid-for announcement can be made in *The Times* for a guinea.

He arranges for a young Frenchman, who has worked for him before, to go to London and use his office while planning an advertising campaign for the hotels, and he tells the young man to be careful not to interfere with the other clerks. He expresses gratitude to Victor Rey (by then at the Carlton, in London) for having refused an offer for his services from D'Oyly Carte although 'it was very seductive'. He receives three brace of pheasants from the Duke of Orleans and writes to thank him, adding, 'We drank a glass of champagne to his health'. He sends a friend in London a recipe for *Sole Paprika* and apologises for not translating it into English as there are 'so many technical words'.

He is trying to sell his house at Golders Green and telling the gardener not to plant too much for next season but just to keep the place looking as nice as possible. He also promises him a £10 bonus when the house is sold. He tells a Paris shop to send a box of Mexican tea to a friend. He is planning in detail a double-page advertisement in the *New York Herald* for Easter.

[65]

When he receives the accounts from Salsomaggiore he notes 'the very sensible economies made', sends the manager his congratulations and the chef his compliments. Is the fire insurance in order? Is there plenty of ice in reserve for the summer? Has the housekeeper found a new first needlewoman yet?

The passionate absorption in detail, the zest (although it can only be verbal), the fastidiousness, the courtesy and kindness, are all in those letters.

The book ends with a letter in which he complains of tiredness and says he is waiting impatiently for the sun. Yet in the last sentence of all he is wondering if Mr Harmsworth (Lord Northcliffe) would be inclined to accept an article for the *Daily Mail* about Salsomaggiore, and suggesting that he should go to see the newspaper proprietor about it at Beaulieu.

*   *   *

The only other written relic of César Ritz is a red leather exercise book on the first page of which there is written in bold and beautiful calligraphy, 'MES PLANS—MES IDÉES'. There are no dates anywhere and, except for what is written in a neat secretarial hand, it is almost entirely illegible.

The tragic gulf between Ritz's intentions and his waning powers is summed up in the contrast between the unfulfilled list of contents and the increasingly indecipherable scrawls scattered among the many blank pages of the book. The planning is typical of the meticulous Ritz. The contents list is numbered, allowing various numbers of pages for each heading. These headings are such as 'The Cairo Hotel', 'Marseille', 'Table Decorations', 'Invitations for Cairo', 'Ritz Development', 'Construction of Hotels', 'Provisional Receipts of Hotels', 'Palais des Fêtes'. Two additions to the list, in Ritz's own hand, are '*Memoir*' and '*Discours*'. The latter is a succession of scrawls, apparently unrelated words and phrases, which continues for four pages. All that can be deciphered are names and places. The 'memoir' is little better—three pages of bold, wild scribbles—but from the disjointed words and phrases which can be deciphered there are faint clues to a man noting impressions and opinions, presumably for expansion later. But we shall never know what Ritz had in mind when he jotted down such things as: '*Joie de vivre—belle-mère alsacienne. Hongroise voluptueuse. Americaines plus intelligentes. Anglaises distinguées.* Asquith. Duc Connaught. *Mes plans*—Paris—*bois* avenue—Palais—Opera—English, French, German, Russian. Marie *délicieuse gifteé.* Melba—*gourmet.*'

Perhaps the most pathetic fragment of all is a pasted-in sheet of paper on which is drawn in ink, as a child might draw it, a severe, rectangular building on stilts, which even by today's standards would be strikingly modern. Above it is scrawled, '*Terrain* 100,000. Construction hotel 1,500,000.'

César Ritz was still building, not castles in the air but hotels.

*   *   *

There was a brief spell when hope rallied, and Ritz was able to make a 'recuperative' trip to Egypt. There his wife and friends were delighted to see him evince interest in plans the Ritz Development Company had for an hotel in Cairo.

Back in Paris he showed some interest in the building of the London Ritz, particularly in importing the American idea of an all-steel structure—the first in England. But he relapsed again; lassitude and melancholia set in. He did not delude himself; 'I am worse than a dead man,' he said once, 'for my working life is ended.' His memory began to fail. He shut himself up and brooded. For some years he lived at St Cloud and when his health permitted he read history, tried his hand at clay modelling, played chess and made a pathetic attempt to write his memoirs. But, as Mme Ritz wrote later, he 'gradually sank out of life. A dark cloud seemed to envelop his mind. It lifted only at brief intervals during the fifteen years that elapsed before death released him.'

He spent his last years in a clinic at Küsnacht, near Lucerne, during the First World War. His wife, only thirty-four when Ritz had his first breakdown, was now plunged into the business of running a great hotel. In 1918 their younger son René died of meningitis at the age of twenty-one. Later that year—a few weeks before the armistice—Mme Ritz received a message from her husband's doctor to come at once. It took her two days to get the necessary permission to travel to Switzerland and when she arrived Ritz was dead.

*   *   *

There are few people still alive who knew César Ritz at close quarters in his prime. His son Charles, although only a boy when his father fell ill, is one of the few. His memories and impressions are vivid and, together with what Charles inevitably learned about his father from his mother, they provide a picture of a man some- what different from the twenty-four-hour-a-day hotel genius, one-track tycoon and high priest of efficiency—part autocrat, part automaton—that might be imagined.

The picture is of a sensitive, imaginative, inquiring, receptive man; dedicated, dynamically industrious yet full of fun. He loved children and was especially good at playing with them. (Children are the best witnesses to this quality. Apart from Charles Ritz's testimony, Hans Elmiger, who was Pfyffer's nephew and later a manager of the Ritz for many years, remembers César as the 'nicest, kindest' man he ever knew as a child.) César's fun was simple. Whenever the family was on the way to Switzerland—which César always regarded as 'going home'— and the train drew into Basle he would lean out of the window and shout, 'Where is the porter with the red nose?' All the porters came running and grinning. They all knew M. Ritz and neither he nor they ever tired of this greeting, the point of which was that *all* the Basle porters had red noses. In those days the trains were few and the porters spent their time and their tips in the canteen.

People, almost more than the paraphernalia of hotels, were Ritz's most intense interest. He rated handling people above all qualities for the good hotelier. He had a wonderful memory for faces and names and his instinct for sizing people up in the time it took to shake a hand or exchange a courtesy was apparently infallible. It was said of him that he knew the right treatment for a new guest by the time he was seated at his table. He told his waiters, 'You must gain the confidence of the guest. He may have come in a bad mood, ready to find fault. He may even want a fight. There are several hurdles to be cleared if he is going to relax and enjoy the hotel and his food, and the first of them is for him to like you.'

This intuitive gift, the essential psychology of the career to which he dedicated himself, extended beyond people to situations. He knew his business so thoroughly that he could size up a proposition—the potential of an hotel, for instance—almost at a glance. He did not want, or need, to see the books; he could sense how things were going and when others checked they usually found he was right. If he started on an enterprise and it didn't work as he had reckoned it would he dropped it without hesitation and without a backward glance.

He was quick-tempered over imperfections—a stain or something disarranged was anathema to him, and nothing escaped his eye. When his professional standards were offended he could be formidable indeed. Hans Elmiger told me, 'He could take the knife from a maladroit carver and threaten him with it. He would be like a lion, his eyes inflamed with rage.' But the storm quickly blew over and nothing was left behind; no recriminations, no rancour. And the same man always gave an employee three chances before firing him. But although quick himself and impatient of slowness in others he always examined a situation from all angles. He would seek information and suggestions from anybody before announcing a decision he had probably made in the first minute. But he had to confirm it by logic. Once a decision, based on a realistic assessment, was made he never wavered. He would, Charles Ritz considers, have made a great general because his equipment was realistic logic, quick perceptions, intuition, decisiveness and speed of thought. He hated unnecessary complications. For all the grandeur with which his name is associated he was essentially modest and simple, and simple logic was the basis of all his thinking.

The combination of orderliness and a passion for scrupulous cleanliness produced side-results which might have been mistaken for vanity. César was a notably well-dressed man, though not a dandy. He thought his appearance was of great importance to his hotel. He bought his clothes in eights, one set for each day of the week and one for special occasions. A 'set' meant four outfits for each day, formal and informal, to be worn according to the time of day and the occasion. He bought his silk top-hats eight at a time too, and his shoes and ties by the dozen. Although not tall, he carried his clothes—as his wife noted from that early photograph as a young waiter—with ease and distinction. He always wore a flower in his buttonhole and he dressed his moustaches daily with Pomade Hongroise.

The highly personal note he gave to his hotel (and to those he managed earlier) did not mean that he saw himself as a one-man show. He was constantly on the look-out for good men to work for and with him, and he had a flair for finding and combining them. Once he had spotted a man he would not rest till he got him. 'A good man is beyond price' was one of his maxims. Escoffier is the supreme example of his flair for talent-picking and his manager and *maître d'hôtel*, Elles and Olivier (who, with Mme Ritz, were the first to have to carry on his work when he no longer could) are held by those who knew them to be a perfect example of hand-picked teaming. Both were simply waiters when he found them. All his subordinates were disciples, devoted to him, though he worked them hard but no harder than he worked himself.

Not only could he delegate, but, far ahead of his time, he believed in daily staff conferences. All heads of departments (except the accountants) were present and were invited to speak freely. The absence of money-men was part of Ritz's belief that hotel management and book-keeping should not be too closely linked. In fact he himself provided the link. He never wanted to know the details. He required only the key figures. Again his 'feel' of how the hotel was going was usually accurate.

Ritz could not visit a place without planning an hotel there. He anticipated the modern hotel tycoon in that much as he cherished his original Ritz he was always aiming to build up a chain of hotels around the world, and, considering the limitations of the time, his travelling on hotel enterprises was prodigious.

Ritz never fussed about money, except that he could not

abide economies that affected quality. He was always forward-looking, for all his love of tradition. 'I know what guests want today,' he would say, 'but what will they want tomorrow?'

His only interest in making money was that it would enable him to make more and better hotels, and he would rather drop profits than standards. Money was important only in helping him to accomplish his mission.

He had an excellent palate for food and drink, but ate sparingly and drank very little, especially by the standards of the times he lived in. He loved fitness, and, busy as he was, he would find time to go riding for exercise.

He was always accessible to everybody, a good listener and just, tending only to be too kind.

Everything interested him, not only in the hotel business. He was fascinated by any new enterprise even if it was quite unconnected with his world and there was nothing in it for him. He was always helping people with advice and money.

It is difficult now to appreciate some of the problems he had to tackle. Many things now common in hotel or domestic equipment were not made in his time. When he had an idea he had to work it out in practical design and detail and then find somebody to make it for him—whether it was a particular lock or light-fitting or a cooking or serving utensil.

He was devoted to his wife and his greatest private pleasure was to get her to sing for him. But he was no pliant spouse whose wife could do no wrong. He could apply his skill in handling people to Marie-Louise. He, the manager *in excelsis*, sometimes thought that she, who shared his perfectionism, was 'too managing'; he never failed to tease or joke her out of it, and never had a row. It is rare indeed for the dedicated career man to be in his home (as his widow's memoir makes it clear he was) an ideal husband too.

CHAPTER FOUR

AFTER RITZ

THE LOSS to the Ritz through the disappearance of its creator from the active scene only four years after it opened was, of course, immeasurable. But thanks to César Ritz's capacity for inspiring others and leading them in his ways there were trained hands and minds ready to carry on.

Mme Ritz had, of course, been brought up in the hotel business, and she devoted her married life to helping her husband in every way she could; her close participation in his work was remarkable for a woman of the Victorian age who also had to run a home and bring up two boys. When her husband fell ill she joined the board of directors and until she was nearly eighty she continued to have supervisory responsibility in matters of decoration and house-keeping; her taste and her expert knowledge of such things as fabrics, carpets and linen were of immense value.

Ritz's ability to pick men to work for and with him has already been mentioned; it is amply demonstrated by the significant fact that in the sixty years since Ritz's collapse the management of the hotel has been in the hands of only four men: Henry Elles, Victor Rey, Hans Elmiger and Claude Auzello, the first two of them César's protégés and the others thoroughly imbued with the Ritz spirit and methods by years of working closely with them. Hans Elmiger (who worked under Rey and Auzello) has said that Ritz's teaming of Elles and Rey 'amounted to genius' and that they, with Auzello, should be credited with having achieved the seemingly impossible—to run the Ritz without Ritz but as Ritz would have wanted it.

When César took some of the stars of his staff, including Escoffier and Elles, to London in 1899 to help him launch the Carlton he had strong reserves to carry on in Paris, notably Rey (promoted from reception), Gimon, who became head chef, and Olivier, who was to become one of the most famous of *maîtres d'hôtel* and remained in charge of the Ritz restaurant for nearly forty years. Certainly in the pre- and post-First-World War periods Olivier was the best-known name among the Ritz staff.

Olivier Dabescat emerges as almost a prototype Ritz man. He was a perfectionist, a model of courtesy and tact. He was dedicated to the ideals which César had established; no job was too small for his attention and he could mingle with the famous on whatever terms they chose without being over-impressed or losing any of his dignity. The essence of his character seems to have been that he simply wanted to be the perfect *maître d'hôtel*—no more and no less. He had total authority and yet remained modest. He declined—politely evaded might be the more apt word—repeated offers of honours and decorations from foreign royalties because they had for him no connection with his job. He consistently refused to be made a member of the Légion d'Honneur because it seemed to him inappropriate. The greatest honour he could conceive was to be known as the king of *maîtres d'hôtel*. When he was promoted to be director of the Ritz restaurants he made a condition—that he should be allowed to keep his style of dress. He would not contemplate giving up the uniform of *maître d'hôtel*.

Olivier's career began at the Bristol Hotel in London at the age of twelve and as a waiter at the exclusive Amphitryon Club he served and got to know the Prince of Wales, Lord Salisbury, Lord Rosebery and Mr Gladstone. He returned to his native Paris to work at the then world-famous restaurant Paillard and it was there that Ritz spotted him.

Madame Ritz records that Olivier became 'almost a stock figure in literature'. 'No fashionable lady,' she says 'felt her

[73]

memoirs to be complete without anecdotes of Olivier of the Ritz.'
He was portrayed on the stage under the name of Antoine by
Edouard Bourdet in the play *Le Sexe Faible*. The play is set in a
luxury hotel and Antoine is the pivot around which the involved
comedy of amorous and cynical intrigue revolves. Everybody
confides in him and seeks his advice with their problems. He is
the essence of tact; dignified, discreet, indeed the only really
admirable and solid character in the play. He enters into intrigue
on behalf of his feckless or venal clients, but always with delicacy
and he never puts a foot wrong. He even chides those who would
go what he considers too far in their confidences and their
schemes, but he always 'keeps his place'. Indeed at the end of the
second act he offers the play's only criticism—and that by implica-
tion—of all that the author is quietly ridiculing. When somebody
says good-night to him and asks if he is going home now,
Antoine replies that he is going for a walk.

'For exercise?'

'For a little fresh air,' he gravely replies.

Olivier saw the play, watched the actor, Victor Boucher, give
what everybody else knew to be an impersonation of him, and
completely failed to recognise himself in the character.

One of Olivier's most prized possessions was a complete set of
the works of Marcel Proust, inscribed, '*A mon ami Olivier*'.
Proust was a familiar figure at the Ritz, so much so that when at
long last his great novel began to appear and receive ecstatic
reviews some of his friends said incredulously, 'What? Marcel
Proust? Little Proust of the Ritz?' He celebrated the success of
the book with a series of dinner parties at the hotel.

His friendship with Olivier extended beyond his visits to the
restaurant. Sometimes he came late at night and dined alone in a
private room. He was served personally by Olivier, who had seen
to it in advance that the fire was exactly right (Proust was always
complaining that fires were too hot or not hot enough) and that
every chink of windows and doors had been carefully padded to
keep out any possible draught that could worry the hyper-
fastidious, hypochondriac semi-invalid. Proust and Olivier were
sometimes seen on summer evenings walking in the Bois, deep

in conversation, but, typical of Olivier, no one ever learned what they talked about.

André Maurois says that when, after Proust's mother died and his entertaining was done in restaurants, it was 'preferably the Ritz—whose *maître d'hôtel*, Olivier Dabescat, with his air of discreet distinction, simple dignity and knowledge of how such things ought to be done, enchanted him'. Now living in a furnished flat, Proust wrote to a friend asking for advice on selling some of his possessions he no longer required: 'I have a vast amount of table silver which I never use because either I eat at the Ritz or lie in bed drinking coffee.'

Maurois describes an occasion when Proust took endless trouble to arrange a dinner for Calmette, the editor of *Figaro*:

'At long last the dinner actually took place, in a private room at the Ritz, panelled in cerise brocade and filled with gilded furniture. Considerable surprise was caused by the presence, in this scheme of decoration, of "two furred and padded Lapps", who turned out to be Proust and Mme de Noailles. Risler, engaged at the last moment, played Wagnerian overtures. Dinner done, the tips had to be distributed. Marcel wanted to give Olivier 300 francs, but the guests flung themselves upon him in an effort to modify his generosity. He promptly gave more.'*

Another Ritz story of Proust's sudden bursts of generosity is of an occasion when he borrowed 100 francs from the hall porter, then handed the money back to the man, saying, 'That's what I wanted it for.'

Proust's excursions into entertaining at the Ritz, says Maurois, 'were in the nature of sudden attacks planned to bring him information about the enemy, in other words, the outside world. . . . He went out less and less, but his seclusion was never absolute, except during his bad attacks. He was to be seen still, supping alone at the Ritz, with almost all the lights out, surrounded by waiters whom he had trained to manipulate the switches, the positions of which he knew by heart.'

* *The Quest for Proust* (Jonathan Cape, 1950).

Of this period of Proust's life Dr Milton L. Miller writes: 'Sometimes he went out at 2 a.m. to see if anyone was still attending a dinner party he had ordered to be given at the Ritz.'*

In 1922 Proust wrote to his friend the Duc de Guiche, 'Nothing amuses me less than that which was called twenty years ago "select". What does amuse me are the many mixed parties and gatherings which are like firework displays. I get that from the Ritz.'

'He was certainly attracted by this carefully guarded world,' the Duke wrote later, 'a world which could afford to be gay, for it had no material worries and often gave delightful parties. It is perhaps difficult, in speaking of his excursions into the fashionable world, to distinguish Proust the voluptuary from Proust the naturalist.'

In another letter to Guiche, Proust hopes they may have dinner together at the Ritz 'where the staff is so obliging that I feel at home and am less tired'. Arranging a dinner with Guiche, via a long letter to his personal servant, full of detailed and alternative arrangements for what is really a simple social date, Proust says, 'The only condition I impose is that it shall be at the Ritz, as, not being at all well, I prefer to be where there is no jostling.'†

Proust was a compulsive and voluminous letter-writer. To Sir Philip Sassoon, who was staying at the Ritz, he wrote:

'For a long time I have heard nothing of you except the murmur of the water running into your bath. I was dining at the Ritz (where I often take a room for a few hours) and, believing I had no neighbours, I was telling a waiter who had learned the part of Sosie for the Conservatoire of what Molière's play consisted (the Conservatoire having rejected him and thus sent him back to his old profession at the Ritz). Suddenly threatening noises were heard from next door and the sound of a perfect deluge; I did not doubt that, in punish-

* *Nostalgia: a Psychoanalytical Study of Marcel Proust* (Houghton Mifflin Co.; Boston, 1956).

† *The Veiled Wanderer*, by Princess Marthe Bibesco (Falcon Press, 1949).

ment for my irreverent explanations, Jupiter was letting loose his thunder. But no, I was told that it was Sir Philip Sassoon taking his bath.'

Sir Harold Nicolson occasionally dined with Proust at the Ritz, always at the table near the door which Olivier surrounded with draught screens, in spite of which Proust still wore his heavy overcoat. Nicolson recalls Olivier solicitously asking if the draughts had been excluded, to which Proust replied, 'There is always a draught for me, my dear Olivier, but your kindness diminishes it.'

Towards the end of his life, Proust lived largely on a diet of coffee and milk, but 'occasionally (though very rarely) he felt a longing for fried sole or roast chicken, and these dishes he had sent round . . . from the Ritz hotel'. When he was dying he refused to take any food and his maid, Céleste, recorded that 'the only thing he could fancy was iced beer, which Odilon (his taxi-driver) was told to get in from the Ritz'. On the morning of the day he died he sent for some beer. He whispered to Céleste that it would be with the beer as with everything else—it would come too late. But it didn't. Improbably enough, his last-but-one utterance was the polite but prosaic sentence, 'Thank you, my dear Odilon, for fetching the beer.'

In the pre-1914 days Olivier was greatly in demand, helping and advising hostesses with dinner parties in their own homes—a labour of love on his part, and there is no doubt his generosity was greatly exploited. Sometimes, however, the whole dinner party was organised from the Ritz. There was a celebrated occasion when Mrs William Corey, who had a château outside Paris, engaged Olivier to cater for a fancy dress party of 150 people for dinner and 250 for supper. Olivier sent the food, kitchen utensils and waiters in five vans. Dinner was served at ten o'clock, followed by fireworks, dancing and music, and champagne supper was served at three a.m. The party broke up after dawn and it was seven o'clock before Olivier's duties were finally over. He recalled with admiration that when the indomitable hostess thanked him and said, 'You must be tired' (which he was) she announced that she was going to have a bath and go riding as it was a lovely morning.

Olivier and Gimon were very different types and the violence of their quarrels—the seniority of chef and *maître d'hôtel* is always arguable—is still remembered, though they took place well away from the guests. Gimon was a supreme chef, but he did not have Olivier's modesty. Reminiscing about Ritz, he once said, 'He often used to come to the kitchen to compliment me'. Mme Ritz asked if he was sure it was always compliments. 'But yes,' said Gimon, astonished, 'M. Ritz never had cause for complaint so far as I was concerned.' Olivier on the other hand always spoke of Ritz with awe, perhaps because Olivier himself was a perfectionist, with an eye which missed nothing. 'If something was well done he was the first to notice it,' he said of Ritz. 'But if something was badly done he was a veritable lion.'

There is something about the concentration of hotel life which, in an innocent, even endearing way distorts values. The world of the hotel becomes more important than the world outside. Mme Ritz gives a revealing instance of this when, writing of Proust and other authors who presented their works to Olivier, she says, 'There have been and are many great writers, but there is only one Olivier.'

Courteous and generous though he was, Olivier was also undeniably a snob. When Mme Ritz once asked him who had been the guests at a large and fashionable party for which he had made the arrangements, Olivier shrugged and said, '*Tout* Paris.'

Olivier made friends in high places and he was prepared to make use of them. During the First World War it was forbidden in Paris to serve alcohol to Allied officers on leave. At the Ritz the rule was quietly broken by Olivier, who felt that if men were risking their lives it was only right that he too should take a little risk. Anticipating the tricks of American prohibition, he served whisky and champagne in teapots. The authorities inevitably heard of this and a summons was served on the management. The prospect was that the hotel might be closed. Olivier immediately went to see Georges Mandel, then *chef de cabinet* to

Clemenceau, the Prime Minister. Mandel was one of those Ritz
habitués whom Olivier could count as a friend. Mandel immediately picked up the telephone, called the police and said,
'Please cancel this summons', and that was that.

Mandel stayed at the Ritz for many years, including the period
between the wars. He kept one of his rooms in permanent near-
darkness, for he disliked lights and draughts. His offices at the
ministries over which he presided were always dim and suffocat-
ing. He had other eccentricities. His appearance was such that on
one occasion when he was due to dine with General Sir Edward
Spears (Churchill's liaison officer with the Reynaud government)
it was found that he had been shown into the servants' hall. He was
economical by nature and his socks were often darned until there
was nothing more to darn. A chambermaid told this to Mme Ritz
who from then on bought new, identical socks and replaced them.
He never knew—or at least never admitted knowing.

In November 1939 Churchill and Mandel dined at the Ritz
and Mandel said firmly that the sooner Churchill took charge of
the war for Britain the better it would be for everybody. He
remained the strong man of the Reynaud government and though
he could have escaped from Bordeaux after the fall of France and
the overthrow of the Government he did not do so and was
arrested by the new regime of Marshal Pétain. He was imprisoned, later handed over to the Germans, returned by them to
Vichy, and eventually murdered soon after the Allied invasion in
1944.

General Spears tells* how Mandel's mistress, Mlle Bretti, of the
Comédie Française, remained loyally by his side as long as
possible and he thinks that in those last black days she married
him. She was a close friend of Mme Ritz and, after the war, it
was she who pinned the ribbon of the Légion d'Honneur on
Mme Ritz, an honour of which she was very proud.

Olivier was one of the few people who knew Calouste Gulbenkian, the oil millionaire, well. Once, and only once, Olivier
asked him for advice about certain shares, whether to buy or sell.
The shares did the opposite of what Gulbenkian predicted and

* *Assignment to Catastrophe* (Heinemann, 1954).

Olivier was very surprised. But he later discovered that Gulbenkian always told people who asked for advice the opposite of what he would do himself. It was a very effective technique of discouragement.

*   *   *

Olivier, even when in the exalted position of restaurant director, continued to follow the practice of *maîtres d'hôtel* (and even the great hostesses of the time) who, while they would order all the rest of the food to be served at the table, would personally shop for their fruit. As long as he was at the Ritz, Olivier went to the market and chose the fruit himself, as his successors, Sénéchal and Paul, continue to do today.

'A menu concocted by Olivier is a *chef-d'œuvre*', Mme Ritz said. One of the most celebrated dinners he arranged was for a party of ten men. The host was celebrating the conclusion of a successful deal. He went to Victor Rey, then the manager of the Ritz, and said, 'Money doesn't matter. I only want you to see that the food and wine are perfect.' He gave Rey 10,000 francs on account. By the time Rey, Olivier and Gimon had arranged the dinner, the host was in their debt for another 2,000 francs. (The franc then stood at about 123 to the pound. Thus, the cost of the dinner was approximately £10 per head, but to arrive at a present-day comparison that figure has to be multiplied by about four.)

The menu and the wine list that Olivier served on that occasion are worth recording:

Consommé de faisan en tasse

Mousseline de sole Empire
Cassolette de queues d'écrevisses

Escalope de foie gras au beurre noisette
Velouté de petits pois frais

Carré de veau brasé à la crème
Pommes de terre Anna
Pointes d'asperges

Sorbets au Montrachet

Bécasses au fumet
Salade de laitue
Truffes en papillotes
Mandarines de Nice givrées
Friandises
Les plus beaux fruits de France

Sherry Carta Oro Viejo
Meursault Goutte d'Or 1915
Château Léoville-Barton 1878
Château Lafite 1870
Pommery 1911
Grand Chambertin 1906
Romanée 1881
Giesler 1906
Château d'Yquem 1869
Cognac Hennessy (Réserve Privée)

The claret and the Château d'Yquem were specially brought from Bordeaux by a messenger who sat up all night in the train with the bottles in his hands to ensure the minimum vibration. The dinner lasted from eight-thirty until eleven and the party did not break up until two o'clock in the morning. Rey recorded with pride that the host telephoned each of his guests next morning and was assured that none of them had any after-effects.

*　　*　　*

Olivier could nod. Sir Harold Nicolson, walking one morning in the Rue de Rivoli, met Captain Edward Molyneux, the couturier, who asked him to lunch. Nicolson accepted, but added, 'Only if we go to the Ritz. Olivier is the only head waiter who knows me, and I enjoy that.' They went to the Ritz and Olivier greeted them, but addressed Molyneux: '*Bonjour, mon capitaine, comment allez-vous?*' At last he turned to Nicolson and said politely, 'Mr Bonstetten, is it not?' This exception to the stories of Olivier's phenomenal memory delighted Molyneux, and Nicolson is too modest a man not to have laughed at it too. 'I have never seen a man,' said Molyneux, 'so gratuitously make himself look foolish', and Nicolson could only agree.

When Sir Harold was in Paris for a conference in 1919 with his chief, Lord Curzon, the Foreign Secretary, they returned late one night from the Quai d'Orsay. It had been arranged that supper should be ready. Olivier seated them and then said anxiously to Lord Curzon, 'The last time you had supper you had an omelette. I remember I gave you a kidney omelette but I cannot remember if you liked it or not.' Before Curzon could reply, Olivier produced a dish and added, 'So to be sure I have prepared two omelettes, one kidney, so that you shall have what you prefer.'

'Olivier,' says Sir Harold in 1963, 'was the Napoleon of *maîtres d'hôtel.*'

In a memoir written thirty-five years ago, Nicolson described one of those after-conference suppers at the Ritz: 'I remember Olivier ministering to Lord Curzon and yet not ignoring us— Olivier blending with a masterly precision the servile and the protective, the deferential and condescending.'*

One of Sir Harold's memories of the Ritz is of an early morning departure with the Foreign Secretary and his entourage. Lord Curzon, in his majestic way, always cut things fine in point of time, never catching a train more than a minute before it was due to leave. The party was ready and waiting when Curzon appeared from the lift, escorted by Elles, 'pale and courtly'. Curzon at that time—and for a brief period (about which Nicolson has written amusingly in *Some People*)—had a drunken valet named Arketall. In eleven minutes they were due at the Gare de Lyon, where M. Poincaré, the Prime Minister, was waiting to accompany them to Lausanne. There was no sign of Arketall. As Curzon, always in pain, climbed into the waiting car and sank back on the seat, he beckoned to Nicolson and murmured, 'I shall want my foot-rest.'

Nicolson dashed back into the hotel. Elles was standing at the foot of the staircase, but before Nicolson could ask if the valet (or the foot-rest) had been seen, there was a bump and an exclamation from above. Round the last turn of the stair came

* *Some People* (Constable, 1927).

Arketall, who was always liable to be unsteady on his feet. He shot round the bend like a bob-sleigh and landed beside Nicolson with his feet in the air and the foot-rest held above his head. 'Crakey', he said.

They arrived at the train with one minute to spare. M. Poincaré, Nicolson thought, looked irritated. As the train slid out of the station Arketall, who was standing close to Nicolson, suddenly said, 'Ay left me 'at behind.' Nicolson says he suddenly had a shaming picture of 'that disgraceful bowler lying on the Ritz stair carpet. They might even think it was *le châpeau de Lord Curzon!*' But he had underestimated the Ritz. A secretary came up at that moment, holding a bowler. 'They threw this into our motor as we were leaving the Ritz', she said.

In those days of more than forty years ago Nicolson recalls the Ritz as the most glittering centre of fashion in Paris, if not the world. He remembers as specially magnificent the dinner parties in the Salon Carré at the time of the Versailles peace conference when, if the French Government was the host, the entrance and stairs were lined by the most splendidly caparisoned of all France's men in uniform, the Garde Républicaine.

One of the most colourful of Ritz residents at that time was Josef Potocki, who gave enormous parties during the conference. Potocki was a Pole and on one occasion Paderewski, then the Polish Premier, was present. Afterwards Nicolson remarked to his host what a fine and charming man Paderewski was. 'Yes,' said Potocki, 'it's remarkable. He comes from one of my villages and, do you know, I find myself talking to him as though he were an equal.'

*　　*　　*

Victor Rey was a true disciple of Ritz, on whom he unconcealedly modelled himself. He too was a Swiss, tactful, courteous, with a lively intelligence and a resourcefulness which was what first brought him to César's notice. While he was a reception clerk the Exposition of 1900 brought to Paris a flood of visitors and the Ritz could not cope with the demands for rooms. Young Rey went to Elles and suggested that, as they did not want people who had to be refused at the hotel to go to other parts of Paris but at least to keep them in the Vendôme-St Honoré neighbourhood, they might co-operate with the near-by hotels.

This was a revolutionary idea as between rival hotels and Elles was doubtful, but he gave Rey permission to try. The result was that the Ritz reception became a clearing house of the supply-and-demand problems of the district. Rey became a multiple receptionist, always armed with a list of what was available at hotels like the Continental and the Lotti and sorting out the accommodation to the best advantage.

While Rey was at the reception desk he had an experience which always amused him to retell. Early one morning the English newspaper magnate Alfred Harmsworth (later Lord Northcliffe) arrived at the hotel. He remarked that Rey looked pale and haggard. Rey tried to pass it off, but Harmsworth insisted on knowing what was wrong and Rey admitted that his wife had been taken to a maternity home during the night and he did not know what was happening; he could not get away for another hour when he would be relieved. Harmsworth immediately went round behind the counter and in spite of Rey's protests packed him off. He had always wondered, he said, what it was like to be on the other side of the fence in an hotel. By the time Rey's relief arrived Harmsworth had received and let rooms to a party of Americans and was highly delighted with himself.

Sizing up new people is a skill hotel men always like to practise and Rey was particularly astute at it. One day he was talking to Olivier when Lady de Grey entered the hotel with a woman neither of them knew. 'I'll wager you she's a queen,' Rey said. She was in fact Queen Sophie of Greece.

When coal was unobtainable in Paris during the First World War, Rey, by then manager, became worried when even the stocks the Ritz had laid in were running low. He sent scouts out into the streets to look for coal delivery carts and to persuade them to divert their deliveries to the Ritz. The result was not only that the hotel was kept warm but Rey was occasionally able to oblige freezing clients with a little coal for their homes.

Another favourite recollection of Rey's was an occasion much later—in the Thirties—when he arranged a party which he considered one of his greatest triumphs, worthy of the 'great days' before the war. The hostess was Barbara Hutton. Rey transformed the dining-room and rooms adjoining into a scene representing Casablanca. The menu was Moroccan and the band was flown from London. About a thousand guests dined at tables each seating twelve or fourteen.

The people who worked with Rey recall him as an exacting task-master but a kind one; like Ritz, he always gave an employee three chances and reprimands were administered in private.

*   *   *

When the 1914 war began the Ritz offered the whole of the first floor to the Government as a hospital for wounded soldiers. The accommodation was soon overcrowded, so the whole of the Rue Cambon building was closed to guests as well and turned into a hospital.

Later, Allied officers on leave were received free at the hotel. This proved so attractive that a time-limit had to be applied; no officer might stay more than three days. Then it was found that some officers were staying three days, going away for a day and checking in again for another three, repeating this operation as long as their leave lasted. Reluctantly the Ritz was forced to make a charge. It seems absurd now, but the charge was the equivalent of seven and sixpence (or a dollar) a day.

For Mme Ritz the war years were, in terms of the beloved hotel and way of life she was accustomed to, a period of oblivion. 'Society found new occupations, new standards, new ideals,' she writes, sadly and revealingly. When she was writing her memoir, nearly twenty years later, she asked Rey to remind her of what had happened at the Ritz in those years. But it was no good; 'M. Rey,' she wrote, 'gave me a complete list of the important events that were held at the Ritz during the war years. He also gave me a list of the important officers who stayed at the hotel either as convalescents or on important missions or as invalids. I have mislaid these lists. And, anyway, I do not seem to be able to recall this epoch with any interest whatever. I remember only

the brooding horror of those years and the events—tragic events
—that affected me personally then.'

She is referring not only to the continued tragic illness of her
husband and his death in 1918 but also to the death of her second
son, René, of spinal meningitis in the same year.

The death of René was a great blow to the Ritz family. Even
when he was a small boy he wrote plays and produced them.
There seemed no doubt that he had a natural talent for the
theatre and that his career would have lain there. The great
comedian, Coquelin (who still has a dish named after him on the
Ritz menu), said the boy had genius, and wanted to take him
under his wing. Sacha Guitry too predicted a great future for
him.

Meanwhile the elder son, Charles, had gone to America in
1916, having already done his military service in the Swiss Army
and served at the Ritz for a time as secretary to the manager,
Elles. Of those teenage days in hotel work M. Ritz recalls two
items. He had just learned to smoke a pipe but was distressed to
find he could not conveniently combine smoking with typing for
M. Elles. One day he was found by the astonished manager
smoking a long clay churchwarden, which he had ingeniously
suspended from the ceiling, while he worked at the typewriter.

But a much more serious problem in young Charles's life as a
secretary was the difficulty he had in taking M. Elles's dictation.
He was sure the manager was quite unaware of how difficult it was,
so he bought a dictaphone, with wax records, and induced M.
Elles to dictate into this. He then played it back to the manager,
who was horrified to hear himself dither and hesitate and
complicate the letters which young Ritz was expected to produce
immaculately. The cure was immediate and complete.

Elles emulated César in the elegance of his appearance. His
model for style was 'the English gentleman'. Like César, his
exercise was riding and Charles Ritz remembers endless letters
he had to write to Elles's London tailors, discussing the details of
his riding breeches.

*   *   *

Charles Ritz speaks with the greatest admiration of his mother's abilities. His greatest pleasure, in her late life, was that she ultimately approved the new Espadon grill-room, although it was quite unlike anything ever done before at the Ritz. She disapproved of the plans for it at first and before it was ready she said, 'You've gone too far. None of our old customers will set foot in the place.' But she came round. 'Even at nearly ninety,' M. Ritz says, 'she was capable of appreciating that it was good and desirable for the hotel, although it was a world removed from her own taste and traditions.'

Mme Ritz's eagle eye was well known and feared. She always ate in the restaurant and watched everybody and everything. 'Every damn thing,' her son said to me one day recently, still marvelling. 'She had a terrific eye. She was the most critical person I have ever known. If a waiter dropped a plate at the other end of the room she jumped and made a face as if she had been hurt.' He chuckled. 'One day when this happened I could not resist saying, "Mother, you mustn't let everybody know so clearly you *own* the plate."' He paused for a moment and shook his head. 'Her very strict methods would be impossible now, and personally I'm glad of it. But things may have gone too far the other way. Anyhow, everything my mother did was for the good of the hotel.'

Janet Flanner, the Paris correspondent of the *New Yorker*, retains a vivid, characteristic picture of Mme Ritz: 'She came into the dining-room hatted, gloved and parasoled, although she was in her own home. Every male form rose from its chair a little as she passed. The gentlemen bowed; Madame bowed. The more important waiters pushed the minor waiters behind them so that they themselves could make the deepest bow. She acknowledged the bows regally, yet one knew her eye was taking in everything everywhere.'

Mme Ritz lived in the hotel through two wars. A picture of her as she was during the second is given by Louis Bromfield in his *What Became of Anna Bolton*. Although the book is fiction, Mme Ritz is identified by name and the description of her and her background is the work of Bromfield the reporter rather than

Bromfield the novelist. Describing Paris at the time of the collapse of France in 1940 he writes, 'But inside the Ritz life went on as usual. . . . Mme Ritz gave stability to the whole establishment. There were many people who did not believe in her existence—that there could be a Madame Ritz—or they thought that if there had been she must long since be dead. Many of them had seen her, small, white-haired, chic, with her two Pekinese* at her heels, going quietly about the big hotel, never knowing that she was the widow of the great César Ritz, that she was in her own right a great woman.

'She lived quietly in a comfortable suite of rooms beneath the mansard, surrounded by her Pekinese and countless canaries in cages, a woman full of wisdom and utterly without illusions.

'Each day she made a round of the whole establishment from kitchens to linen cupboards, visiting rooms to see that they were properly cleaned and in order. Beneath her there existed a whole staff of officers . . . and all of them had been with her for many years because they felt as she felt about the Paris Ritz. It had always been and must continue to be the best, most luxurious hotel in the world, and the model for all others.'

Later Bromfield describes Mme Ritz in her 'little salon' at the top of the hotel: 'Here on the garden side away from the street there were no sounds. The big trees came almost to the level of the little windows with the lace curtains and little pots of geraniums on the ledge. Up here, beneath the roof, one had no sense of being in Paris. The little room was more like a room in a house in Colmar or Mulhouse or Strasbourg, in the country from which Madame Ritz had come long ago as a little girl. Here, away from all the gilt and mirrors and crimson carpet, Madame Ritz was herself, the innkeeper's daughter from Alsace who knew how to run a fine inn and cared about nothing else in the world.'

Mme Ritz's personal maid, Emilie, who was with her when she died in 1961, told me that even in her final weeks when she was confined to bed she had the daily list of arrivals brought to her and that her memory of individuals and their tastes remained

* In fact Mme Ritz did not have Pekinese but Belgian griffons.

'impeccable'. She could still discuss details of the hotel because she knew each room and its furnishings by heart.

Until the end of her life she took the greatest care with her *toilette* and Emilie attended to her curls every day. She dressed as though for a social occasion and took her meals in the restaurant. As long as it was possible she went downstairs because, she said, the guests should see her. Such things were part of her dedication to the memory of her husband, her determination that the personal Ritz touch should still be made manifest.

Her passion was for quality in all things. If something was done not quite right she would have it done over and over—or started again from scratch—until it was right. Only perfection was permissible. Everything had to be as nearly as possible as in César's time, or as he would have liked it. 'Her whole life was the hotel,' Emilie said. 'She was a hotelier to her fingertips—and beyond.'

It is impossible to tell whether it was the reporter or the fiction-writer in Bromfield who put words into Mme Ritz's mouth. For example, when she is explaining why she intends to remain in Paris when the Germans are approaching, she says, 'For me it does not matter. I won't live to see the end of it in any case. This is my hotel. My husband and I made it. It is our immortality. Three hundred years from now the name Ritz will be a name meaning what it means everywhere in the world.'

CHAPTER FIVE

THE ANCHOR MAN

THE MAN who has run the Ritz for the last twenty-five years—
and has been in its management for eighteen years more than
that—is a Frenchman, the first non-Swiss to be in charge of the
hotel. The holder of such an office might easily be pictured as
the prototype hotelier: smooth, elegant, adept at the slight bow
and the deferential smile. The true picture is almost startingly
different. Claude Auzello, whom Charles Ritz has called 'the
anchor of the Ritz', is essentially a plain man, a seventy-two-
year-old Provençal, solid, somewhat stern-faced and entirely
without frills. With his clipped grey moustache and the rosette of
the Légion d'Honneur in the buttonhole of his conservative dark
suit, he suggests a retired military man rather than the chief
executive of an internationally famous luxury hotel.

He looks considerably younger than his years. His strong face,
with its proud, hooked nose and firm mouth, bears the stamp of
natural and habitual authority; his eyes flash when he is roused
and he admits to a temper over which he has so long practised
control that it shows only when he means it to, and the effect is
quelling. Normally his manner is gravely courteous, but never
even faintly touched by obsequiousness. In private he has a lively
sense of humour and an almost alarmingly loud laugh, which
often comes at the end of a story he has acted out with dramatic
vigour; and when he is with, or speaks of, his American wife,
Blanche, there is a noticeable softening of his whole demeanour.

Auzello's knowledge of and dedication to the Ritz are absolute, yet he has carefully preserved a private life away from the hotel, a life in which he dines at home with his wife most evenings and reads biographies, memoirs and out-of-the-way factual books like a study of feudal taxation. He spends his weekends at his sixteenth-century farm forty miles from Paris where, on twenty-five acres, he raises Friesian cattle and pigs. A drawing of the farm by the late Bryan de Grineau is—apart from the portrait of César Ritz over the fireplace—the principal mural decoration of his office. He keeps a bundle of family and farm snapshots in an elastic band in a drawer of his desk.

On the mantelshelf are two other items, which can hardly be called decoration but are there for a purpose. One is a series of framed bills from the earliest days of the hotel, with the superscription: '*Autre temps, autre prix*'. My first thought when I saw this exhibit was that it would demonstrate how inexpensively one could eat even at the Ritz once upon a time and that such comparison would merely make the present-day visitor nostalgically envious. But Auzello uses it to argue, when the occasion requires, that in fact hotel prices have not risen in proportion to the prices of other commodities and services, that if a fine dinner for one cost, say, £3 in those far-off days it ought to cost £12 now —and it doesn't. The other item which catches the eye in Auzello's office is a blow-up of an extract from the newspaper *Petit Bleu* of October 1940. This is a quotation from the celebrated Cardinal de Richelieu, *éminence grise* and chief minister of Louis XIII, on the subject of French character: 'If our natural misbehaviour often leads us to appalling precipices, our very fickleness prevents our staying there and rescues us with such promptness that our enemies, unable to judge such frequent changes with any accuracy, have not time to take advantage of them.'

One day during the German occupation General von Stulpnagel walked into the office unannounced and caught sight of the panel of print pasted on the mirror by Auzello's desk. He read it, then put his monocle in his eye, and studied the words in silence for what seemed to Auzello a long time. 'He must have read it through carefully two or three times,' Auzello told me. 'There is no doubt about the spirit of the quotation and I wondered if there was going to be any trouble.' At last von Stulpnagel turned to Auzello and, pointing to the date on the cutting, said, 'This was printed quite recently.' 'Yes,' said Auzello. There was a pause. 'Do you believe it?' the German asked at last, expressionlessly. 'From the bottom of my heart,' said Auzello. There was another pause, then Stulpnagel said, 'I congratulate you,' and left the room.

In the general mobilisation of August 1939 Auzello was recalled to the Army. When the collapse came in 1940 he was at Nîmes, in southern France, and it became his task to handle the soldiers who were straggling back from the front. He was dismayed by their fatalistic pessimism and, as a captain, took it upon himself to order several hundred of them to parade in the barrack square and he addressed them from a balcony. His short speech made sufficient impression for a local newspaper, *Le Petit Provençal*, to reproduce it in full:

'Gunners—my friends! As soon as I heard the news of this abominable armistice I thought I must see you immediately because I felt you must be heart-broken.

'I want you to know that nothing is lost. France has seen more tragic moments and she has always risen again.

'The war is only beginning. The Germans are not yet the victors!

'Our ally, England, thanks to her situation, will resist for a long time—and victoriously. Other nations will join her and we ourselves will return to the battle.

'When you get back to your firesides, work, work hard, and keep in your hearts hope and unshaken confidence in our beloved France.'

He was called before his Colonel and asked to explain his conduct. He said that the soldiers had needed a morale-lift and he had simply told them what he knew to be true—what, indeed, should have been told them by somebody else (meaning the Colonel). 'When you are conquered you bow,' said the Colonel.

'Speak for yourself,' Auzello snapped. No action was taken against him.

He was demobilising some 1,500 soldiers a day, giving them papers to show that they were civilians and putting them on the way to their homes. But by September 1940 he decided his job was finished, so he demobilised himself and, knowing it would be futile to ask for official permission to go into the occupied zone, he simply bought a ticket and took a train for Paris. He got through without incident and went straight to the Ritz, entering by the Cambon side, as he knew the Germans were in possession of the Vendôme part. But next day he went through the underground passage to the Vendôme and he was shocked and angry to see some of the staff behaving, as he thought, too servilely. Next day he summoned a staff meeting in the basement and addressed them much as he had addressed the soldiers at Nîmes. But he added a stern instruction for their future conduct to the Germans. 'Service, yes,' he said, 'but nothing more.'

He had brought with him a supply of blank demobilisation forms and his official stamp, and for months afterwards he issued certificates to many Frenchmen who had found their way to Paris but, having no papers, were still in danger of being made military prisoners. (When George, the barman, turned up Auzello 'demobilised' him too and put him back to work at his old job.)

The Germans staying at the Ritz were high-ranking officers and 'guests of the Führer'. The Germans, on the whole, were very 'correct' in their behaviour. By good luck, the Chief of Staff had been a German military attaché in Paris before the war and knew the Ritz well. It was only necessary to remind him that, occupation or no occupation, this *was* the Ritz, and usually difficulties were smoothed out. Auzello determined to be very 'correct' also, but he also determined never to touch a German hand.

One evening he happened to be in the Vendôme lobby when the general who was Military Commander of Paris came downstairs with his entourage. He was going out to dinner and was dressed in all his finery and medals—'a very imposing figure, I admit,' Auzello says. With his procession of aides he was descending the stairway like royalty. Auzello was in his path when he reached the hall. The General smiled and came forward with his hand outstretched. It was a difficult moment and Auzello had only a second to decide what to do. He was dealing with men who had at that time the power of life and death. But he held to his vow to himself, bowed very slightly and walked away. 'For a moment,' he told me, 'I wondered if I had been dangerously foolish over such a little thing. But nothing happened.'

In 1942 the Germans withdrew all the small coinage they could lay hands on and shipped it back to Germany for its aluminium content. This caused a minor but irritating muddle, because it made the giving of small change virtually impossible. The butcher or grocer could give the housewife a scrap of wrapping paper as an IOU in lieu of a few francs change and would honour the credit next time, but the Ritz could hardly do that. Auzello solved the problem by having a quantity of small tin tokens made —round ones for one franc and oblong for two francs. Printed in red were the words: 'Hotel Ritz—*bon pour 2 frs*'. Auzello was careful to lodge with his bank a sum of money to cover the face value of the tokens. But nevertheless he was called before the German authorities. 'You are making false money,' he was told. A handful of the offending tokens was produced. 'You know it is illegal. It says so on your own French banknotes. You can be sent to hard labour for life.' Auzello explained his cash coverage; after all, he was only doing in a small way what every country's Treasury does when it issues money other than gold. But it was no use; he was ordered to withdraw the tokens. It was several months before they ceased to be in circulation, however, and they had served their purpose, as by then the small coinage was drifting back into circulation.

Auzello was soon involved in various kinds of resistance work but he will not talk much about this. 'You never know,' he says, 'there might be another war and I might want to do it all again.' However he is prepared to divulge that the Allies were kept promptly informed of which 'guests of the Führer' were at the Ritz by a simple system he evolved. News of the arrival of a

Göring or a Bormann could be passed by telephone in a few hours to Switzerland. The scheme was based on a numbered list of the German military and political hierarchy. Auzello could pick up the telephone in his office and speak to a business contact in the occupied zone; the resident Germans had no wish to interfere with his organisation of food supplies. The first number he mentioned in the conversation was the significant fact. The contact, by reason of his business, had a permit to cross the line between the zones. On the other side, he telephoned the next link in the chain, a railway man near the Swiss border. This call, from one point within the unoccupied zone to another, was easy enough. The railway man was permitted to telephone across the frontier to Switzerland because he had to exchange messages on traffic. He in turn planted the number in his message—and the job was done.

The Auzellos did not come through the occupation without their troubles. Mme Auzello, lunching at Maxim's one day with a woman friend, remarked on a group at a table near by—two French women lunching with two German officers—saying how she despised such women. A few days later the Germans demanded Mme Auzello's presence at their interrogation headquarters. The result was that she spent four months in prison at Fresnes, convicted of insulting the German Army. Soon afterwards another German posse arrived at the Ritz—an officer and four soldiers, all formidably armed—and announced that Auzello was wanted for questioning. What was he accused of? he asked. Of having Communist associations. Auzello was so relieved he laughed aloud; he had feared they might have penetrated some of his underground activities. 'Me, the director of the Ritz—a Communist?' he said. 'You will make all Paris laugh.' He discovered later that Moscow Radio had commented on the imprisonment of Mme Auzello. What funny people the Germans were, the broadcast said. They made their home at the Ritz and then they sent the boss's wife to jail! The curious German reasoning was that if Moscow knew about this Auzello must be in touch with the Communists.

The Germans began to search through the papers in his office, presumably for evidence of his guilt by association. Auzello's conscience was clear now, but he suddenly realised that among the day's mail on his desk there was an envelope with a New York address on it, which might well be used to establish that he had illicit links with the outside world. While the search was going on he managed to slip the envelope into his pocket. Then he remembered that he had an Army revolver in a drawer—and to have firearms was illegal and punishable. Ostensibly helping the Germans with their search, he was able to slip the gun into his pocket too. The problem now was how to prevent the gun being found on him if, as he expected, he was taken to prison. He told the Germans that if they were going to search they might as well do it thoroughly and search his apartment in town too. He knew his maid was there. While the Germans searched the apartment he contrived to slip the gun to the maid and to whisper to her to put it with the garbage. Also at the apartment he seized a convenient moment to chew and swallow the paper with the incriminating address.

Auzello was questioned for the rest of the day and then put into the Cherche Midi prison at night. He chuckled when he reminisced with me about this. 'You know, it was typically German,' he said. 'They made a great performance of locking me in my cell—big keys clanging and all that. But there was a communicating door into another cell and when my jailers had gone I tapped on it. There was no reply. I turned the handle and went in. The cell was empty—and the door was unlocked. I walked along the gallery, but there were other doors and I saw I couldn't get out, so I went back and shut myself in my own cell and went to sleep.'

He solved very simply the problem of getting information to his wife and to the hotel as to what had happened to him. With his first meal (a bowl of soup; Auzello shudders at the recollection) he was given a piece of hard bread, so he scribbled a message, concealed it in the bread and threw it out of the window in the hope that someone would pick it up. Next morning when he looked out one of his assistants from the hotel was standing on the street and waved to him that all was well. After ten days

Auzello, still uncharged and untried, was released, without explanation.

     *   *   *

Perhaps the most surprising thing for a man with Auzello's background and experience is that he is distinctly anti-snob. As a republican he deplores the use of titles in France and once when an American friend heard him address the Spanish Duke of Alba as 'monseigneur' and asked him why, with his views, he did so, Auzello replied, 'Because I am not obliged to and because he does not insist on it.'

An Englishwoman who had often stayed at the Ritz returned on her honeymoon as the wife of a knight. When a maid said, '*Oui, madame*' she was reprimanded and told to say, '*Oui, milady.*' When this reached Auzello's ears he snorted and said, 'I would have told her that "*madame*" is the most beautiful word in the French language. It was good enough for us to use to our queens. I would have told her that there was once a newspaper poll to decide what was the most beautiful word in the language and "*madame*" won.' Incidentally, he knew that as a knight's wife she was not even technically entitled to 'milady'.

No hotel man's life, even without enemy occupation, ever runs smoothly and in Auzello's years of management there have been two landmark occasions when, by general consent, he saved the Ritz from disaster. Auzello denies this, saying that all he did was to take the logical, practical action necessary in difficult situations.

In the first Blum regime in 1937 the effects of the depression were still being felt and in the hotel business trade was poor and tips meagre. In the radical enthusiasm for the Popular Front a campaign against tips, and for higher wages, gradually grew to a crisis. It was decreed that every place of business should have a house committee composed jointly of labour and management. Auzello presided over the Ritz house committee, which met every week and, he says, was largely a forum for petty grievances.

Meanwhile legislation was going through for a forty-hour week. This was intended originally for miners, and regulations for other industries and trades were to be decided later on the basis of the strenuousness of the job. It was understood that the plan for hotels was to be a forty-five-hour week plus three hours overtime for cooks and fifty hours plus three hours overtime for others, this to be spread over six days.

By the time the law affecting hotels was passed the second (and stronger) Blum ministry was in power and the law emerged as a fifty-hour week spread over only five days. This might have been tolerable in other businesses, where employees do similar jobs, and would have required an increase in staff of one-seventh, but in hotels, where the jobs are more varied, it meant an overwhelming staff increase; in the case of the Ritz eighty more people would have to have been employed, which, Auzello says, would have bankrupted the hotel.

There were strikes in many Paris hotels. The strikers imitated what was happening in industry where, for instance, motor-car factories were being occupied by the sit-down strikers. At the Ritz things went on reasonably well, but there was one genuine trouble-maker on the house committee. He was a floor waiter, an intelligent man and a good worker, whom Auzello held in real professional esteem. But he knew that there would be no peace so long as this man was in a position of influence. Auzello frankly set out to find a legitimate reason for firing him, which he could only do with the approval of the house committee, on the staff side of which the waiter wielded great power.

Auzello had the man watched and one day it was reported that while on the seven a.m. to one shift he had gone out immediately after serving breakfast. Auzello rang the floor pantry and got no reply. He went to the man's floor and found him absent. He then went to the staff entrance and established that the man had clocked in but had not clocked out. Auzello waited. The waiter came back half an hour later with no good excuse for his absence. Auzello told him he had until 12.30 to resign, otherwise he would be fired—that is, given eight days' notice not to be worked. Auzello added that he was prepared to face the consequences, claiming that, whatever the house committee said, he had acted legitimately, whereas the man had broken his contract.

After 12.45 Auzello telephoned and said, 'Why haven't you kept your appointment with me?' The waiter replied that he had decided not to resign. Auzello knew that something must be brewing, especially as his reiteration of the discharge notice brought no protest or argument. At 1.30, when the restaurants were full and Auzello was having his own lunch, word was brought to him that about a hundred of the staff from the floors and the underground departments (though no cook joined the strikers) were gathered in the lobby and a strike had been declared. The waiter had been busy at his union headquarters, where he was an influential figure, and the union had called a strike. The strikers were following the current fashion by occupying the hotel instead of walking out. They had even closed the grille gate to the Place Vendôme.

Auzello at once went into the lobby and asked what the trouble was. He was told that a waiter had been fired without reason. On the contrary, Auzello replied, he had acted legally; the man had fired himself by a gross breach of contract. He added that the strike was not legal as a week's notice of strike action was required by law. He told the strikers that he would give them until 2.30 for everybody to be back at work, and, counting on their own good sense to prevail, he returned to his lunch.

Auzello had subscribed to an organisation which undertook to supply help in case of physical danger arising from labour troubles, so he now called on them to be ready. Colonel Pfyffer and Rey were very nervous. ('I was nervous too,' Auzello recalls, 'but when I am nervous I am very controlled.') He took his Army pistol out of the safe and put it in his pocket, but as it was weighing down his jacket he took it out again and laid it on his desk. Pfyffer panicked and said, 'For God's sake, you're not going to use that.' Auzello replied, 'I'm sorry, Mr President, but if *you're* prepared to stand for such behaviour, I'm not, and I hope you will do as I say.' He asked for their confidence, including what use he made of his pistol. 'Within an hour I promise you there won't be a striker in the house.'

Pfyffer temporised by saying he would go and talk to the men. Auzello remained in the office and heard Pfyffer being greeted by boos. He then telephoned the Prefect of Police and said, 'We are occupied. I want you to clear the house.' The Prefect demurred: he must refer the matter to his minister. Auzello said, 'I warn you, if the house is not cleared by four o'clock, I'll clear it myself, but there will be bloodshed.'

Soon afterwards ten men arrived from the strike-breaking organisation. They were obviously thugs and Auzello had difficulty in restraining them from going into action straight away. The leader took out his false teeth, put them in his pocket, shaped up like a boxer and said, in effect, 'Let me get at them.' Auzello managed to restrain him.

At three o'clock Auzello told the bodyguard not to move from his office until he sent a signal, and he went out to the lobby. He gave the strikers another chance to disperse, but they refused. He then looked round the gathering and said, 'You have traitors among you. One man here came to me this morning and said whatever happened he was on my side. Now he is with you.' He added that *he*—Auzello—was on nobody's side; he was simply an employee of the house, doing his duty and within the law. He then told the strikers they were all fired. They were showing signs of doubt and hesitation when three police vans, with twenty policemen, arrived from the Préfecture. The strikers, Auzello says, 'melted', without the bodyguard having to come into action at all.

At six o'clock the next morning Auzello stationed himself at the staff entrance and as the ex-strikers arrived he refused admission to all but a few he knew had only been frightened by the leaders. They were taken aback by this and about sixty of them gathered in the Rue Cambon, obviously not knowing what to do next.

Later in the morning Auzello's telephone rang and a voice said, 'This is M. Blum'. Auzello thought someone was playing a joke on him and hung up. But the call came through again and it was the Prime Minister, telling Auzello that he had no right to fire his employees. 'It is not the time for this kind of action. You must be patient,' he said.

'This is not a factory, Excellency,' said Auzello firmly. 'I have made my decision and I am within the law. These men will never work in the Ritz again.'

The situation continued critical and the Bill which Auzello believed meant ruin for hotels passed through the Chamber, where Blum had a strong majority. It remained only for the Senate to pass it into law.

One morning Auzello happened to see a newspaper photograph of a senator from Savoy. He did not know the man, but it struck him that Savoy, being a tourist and holiday district with many hotels, would be particularly hard hit by the new law. He telephoned the senator and an immediate—nine a.m.—appointment was made.

Auzello impressed on the senator what the new law would mean, in hard facts and figures, to his constituents. The Bill was due to come up before the Senate in a few days, so the senator quickly rallied a meeting of about a dozen of his colleagues, and Auzello addressed them. Some were immediately concerned with the hotel business, but politically what was more important was that the Senate was not so strongly pro-Blum as the Chamber and the anti-Government senators were looking for an issue on which they could achieve sufficient unity to put up effective opposition. Now they thought they might have found it.

Briefed by Auzello, several senators made powerful speeches in the debate; the vote went against the Government and Blum resigned. This was Auzello's only excursion into politics; he remains half-amused and half-amazed that he had a hand in bringing down a government.

Strike trouble in the Paris hotels lingered on for some time, however, until Auzello urged upon his fellow-members of the syndicate of hotel managers that they would continue to be exploited until they showed some sign of resistance. Their general attitude was that a closure of hotels was unthinkable and any concession had to be made to avoid that. But Auzello argued that it was better to fight a clear-cut issue when they believed themselves to be in the right, and if necessary to see their hotels close, than to have the strike-threat weapon hanging over their heads indefinitely.

The next time the unions made a demand the employers said they could not meet it, demonstrating that it was economically unreasonable. At once the strike threat was raised, whereupon Auzello said quietly, 'We don't care. We are determined, and the sooner you start your strike the better we will like it.' There was no strike and a settlement was reached.

This stand marked the beginning of the end of labour–management troubles which had plagued Paris hotels for years.

The other occasion when Auzello, in the opinion of many people, 'saved the Ritz' was in the early days of the depression when, following the Wall Street crash, first American and then English custom dropped sharply. For the first time in its history the Ritz had to pause and count costs. For over three decades César Ritz's principle was that if you give the best—with, as his son would say, 'no chiselling'—people will pay for it and you will therefore make an adequate profit. What had never been envisaged was a falling-away of trade for no reason connected with what the hotel had to offer. Ritz could not have imagined a period when his clientele might stay away simply because they were short of money.

The problem was how to economise without damaging the quality and standards on which the hotel prided itself. Such economies as cutting staff could only be insignificant if the hotel was to continue functioning at all; the same applied to the paring of overheads. Auzello saw only one way to make any substantial saving and he tackled it with characteristic vigour. The buying of food for the hotel had always been done—as it is now—through a number of suppliers in the neighbourhood. With apologies to them, Auzello said that the Ritz could no longer afford the middleman's profit. They must buy direct. This, of course, involved substituting someone else's skill as a buyer, and Auzello decided to do the job himself.

With his family background as suppliers to Riviera hotels, and his life-long interest in all forms of food, from the farm to the table, he was well equipped for the job. But it was not easy. He had to get up early enough to be at Les Halles when the markets opened, at 5.30. There was no false dignity about the Ritz manager and as often as not he travelled in from his home at Passy on lorries going to the market. He bought meat, vegetables, fruit and cheese, but in much larger quantities than before. He rented storage space in the markets and engaged a butcher for the hotel for the first time, but even with these expenses he was still buying much more cheaply, without loss of quality. Indeed his meat was apt to be even better, for he knew himself, without taking anybody else's word for it, when a carcase had been bought, how long it had been hung and exactly when it should be right for the table.

For three years he went to the market three days a week, reaching the hotel at eight a.m. and going to work after a quick bath. To keep pace with his managerial duties, he stayed till midnight or after on the nights when he was not going to the market in the morning.

The essential economies were achieved; nobody was able to say that the Ritz standards had gone off; but when trade rallied enough for a reversion to the normal system of buying it was a very exhausted manager who returned to normal business hours.

Auzello insists on regarding himself as a working man and not on the opposite side of a class-barrier from other employees. He therefore believes that any labour–management issue concerned with pay or working conditions should be argued out and adjusted, and that in such cases strike action is legitimate, but when a threatened strike has a political basis he will fight it relentlessly.

When Daladier came back from Munich in 1938 there was an upsurge of industrial action against the Government, organised by trade union politicians who opposed the pact the Prime Minister (and Neville Chamberlain) had made with Hitler over Czechoslovakia. The repercussion of this on the Ritz was that Auzello was informed that the staff of the hotel laundry (a separate establishment) was going out on strike in forty-eight hours. This was a purely political gesture. The workers had no grievance against their employer and, in fact, were the best-paid laundry workers in Paris. Auzello immediately drove out to the laundry in the suburbs and summoned the sixty-eight-strong staff into the courtyard, where he told them why, in his opinion, they had no right to strike for political reasons, and warned them of the consequences.

That was on a Monday; the strike was due to begin on Wednesday. Auzello then instructed a lawyer to go to the laundry at 6.30 a.m. on Wednesday and make a legally attested report on what happened. He also had a poster printed, telling the workers that the strike was illegal, that the management would regard it as a breach of contract, and any striker would be dismissed. He withheld the poster until he received a report from the lawyer that only two old women had turned up for work. He then went to the laundry, paid the two women and sent them home, locked the building and put up his poster, plus the lawyer's affidavit as to what had happened.

Two days later a delegation called on him at the Ritz. When they were shown into his office he recognised the leader as a man whose wife, son and daughter all worked at the laundry. Auzello opened the conversation by asking how much the various members of the family earned. He wrote the figures down, added them up and said, 'That's quite a lot of money to have lost overnight.' Then he added, 'But why have you come to see me?' The leader said, 'We want to know when you are opening the laundry.' 'Never,' said Auzello, adding that arrangements had already been made for the hotel work to go to other laundries. Then, to the mystification of the leader, he said, 'But what I don't understand is who you are and why you have come here.' The reply was, 'We are delegates from the laundry.' 'Oh, no,' said Auzello. 'You cannot be. Since two days ago there has been no laundry, therefore there can be no delegation.'

He kept the laundry closed for a month and then took back the staff gradually. When they were all working again he asked them if they had any grievance. They said no. He had made his point about political strikes and has never had any trouble since.

*   *   *

Claude Auzello did not set out to be an hotel man at all. When he left the Army at the end of the First World War he was (in his own word) 'panic-stricken' to realise that he had reached the age of twenty-nine without having started to make a living.

He had studied law under the famous Maître Labori, who defended Dreyfus, but as soon as he qualified as an advocate he started his military service, and the First World War began before he finished. Thus he spent seven years in the Army, finishing as a captain in command of a battery of trench-mortars which suffered heavy losses and eventually became known as 'the suicide club'.

He was in Germany when his demobilisation was imminent and he faced the problem of finding a civilian career. Through his father's business he knew something of the world of hotels, so he decided to try to enter that, though he had no qualifications. It is in character that he aimed at the top. He got hold of a Paris directory, studied the list of hotels, selected four, and wrote to them. The only reply he received was from M. Elles at the Ritz, saying he had nothing to offer but suggesting that the young man might call in next time he was in Paris. Auzello took the train to Paris at once and was engaged by Elles as a learner-receptionist at a salary of 225 francs (about £8) a month.

He had gained a foothold on the bottom rung of the ladder (but a top-class ladder); it might have been that the rest of his success story would simply be a steady ascent to his present eminence. But not at all. He was disappointed and uncomfortable in the Ritz at first. The senior receptionists ordered him about 'like a groom', he says. 'Run here, run there.' He was, after all, twenty-nine and had recently had 600 men under his command. But he was determined to learn. When his colleagues went home at 6.30 every evening he stayed on and studied correspondence, accounts, everything from which he could find out more about how an hotel worked.

Sometimes M. Elles asked him to copy letters—there were no carbon copies at the Ritz in those days. Sometimes he met trains late at night or early in the morning, or arranged for the reception of late-arriving guests. (He still reveals a little nostalgia for those days when guests arrived *en bloc* off the American boat-train or the Golden Arrow or the Blue Train, at fixed times. The Atlantic boat-trains reached Paris in the early hours and the hotel buzzed with activity. Fires burning and supper tables laid in the rooms at four a.m. were quite normal. But flying has ended all that and people arrive at any hour.)

Auzello learned a lot in this arduous way, and with the things that tried him he was determinedly patient, always remembering the Provençal saying he had never forgotten from the day when his father said to him, 'My boy, in life very often you will have to swallow bitter and spit sweet.' But one day he rebelled. He told his seniors in reception that in future they would do the running, not he. Things were better after that.

From those earliest days at the Ritz, Auzello likes to tell a story he might well have never known had he not been so recently a front-line soldier. One day he saw enter the hotel the famous General Brissaud-Desmaillets, whom he had met as his commander at the battle of Chemin des Dames. The General had come to arrange a luncheon for twenty in honour of a corporal— a tough Burgundian of the redoubtable *Chasseurs à pieds*, which the general commanded—who had captured twenty Germans single-handed one night during the battle.

'Of course', Auzello recounts, 'the corporal had never been in a place like the Ritz before, but he conducted himself very well —not ashamed of his hearty appetite and enjoying his share of all the wines served. But eventually silver finger-bowls were placed on the table—you know, lukewarm water with a slice of lemon in it. The corporal did not know about finger-bowls so he started to drink from his. Some of the young officers smiled, but the General did not smile. He suddenly stood up with his own finger-bowl in his hand and said, "And now one last toast in honour of our brave comrade." He drank the contents of his finger-bowl and all the other officers had to do the same.'

Elles took an interest in the willing Auzello and suggested that he should broaden his experience. He found the young man a job at a small hotel in Monte Carlo. His title was receptionist-cashier, but he had no experience of making out guests' bills; he had never realised that there were hotels which did not have bill-clerks. The result was that he was regularly working from six o'clock in the morning until midnight or two a.m. The proprietor was delighted to unload so much work and responsibility on to the young man, as he liked to spend a good deal of time out of the hotel.

One day, in a bar, an elderly, down-at-heel stranger approached Auzello, scrounging a drink. In the course of conversation it emerged that the stranger was an out-of-work bill-clerk. Auzello seized the opportunity; he was himself earning a thousand francs a month, so he then and there engaged the stranger as bill-clerk at 150 francs a month, out of his own pocket. The relief alone was worth it, as M. Auzello says to this day that he is not good at arithmetic.

The new bill-clerk came to work at nights and Auzello established him behind a screen in the reception office. One night the proprietor came home earlier than usual and caught sight of the stranger. Who was this? he demanded. Auzello had no alternative but to explain what he had done. To his surprise the proprietor was so impressed by Auzello's initiative that he took the man on the pay-roll officially.

After a period in Cannes, he returned to Paris as assistant manager of Claridge's. When the ownership changed in 1922 he was appointed manager. Interested now in securing his future (especially as he had made friends with an American family and wanted to marry their attractive daughter), he asked for a contract. The owners promised him one but somehow managed to procrastinate for three years, by which time Auzello's patience was exhausted. Also he had an ambition to have an hotel of his own.

He found a property he thought ideal—a spacious private house in the Faubourg St Honoré and the Avenue Gabriel, which belonged to two aged sisters who were not on good terms. When he called on the one who lived in the house he was informed by the butler that Madame did not receive foreigners. (This was on account of his Niçois name.) Auzello indignantly sent a message that he was an officer of the French Army, and was admitted.

The old lady was willing to sell, but with two provisions: first, that the money should be paid within two months, and second, that although she and her sister owned the property equally she must receive more money than her sister. They agreed a price of 2,500,000 francs for her share, which left it up

to Auzello to secure the sister's agreement at any price less than
that. But the second sister was a very tough trader. He offered
her two million, being prepared to raise it to anything short of
two and a half. At length it was clear that the old lady was holding
out for two and a half, and he agreed.

Immediately he was sent for by the first sister, who greeted him
with, 'I thought you were a French officer—a man of honour.'
Auzello insisted that he was. But the old lady soon revealed that
she knew exactly what he had undertaken to pay her sister.
Auzello countered with 'But I was about to come to you and give
you another 200,000 francs to keep our bargain.' This satisfied
her.

Auzello formed a ten-million-franc company, with such
backers as Otto Kahn, Senator Marconi and Sir James Dunn,
the Canadian magnate. It now looked as though the project was
a *fait accompli* and but for a totally unforeseeable difficulty the
Faubourg St Honoré might today have its Hotel Auzello and the
Ritz a different managing director.

Building permission was required and now Auzello ran into
every difficulty that French bureaucracy could create. Bewildering barriers were put in his way. One objection was that an hotel
could not be built there because it would be possible to shoot the
President in the gardens of the Elysée Palace. Auzello, the old
soldier, pointed out in vain that, even given the desire to do so,
no living gunman could accomplish such a feat of marksmanship.
He went to pains to discover what underlay the difficulties he
was encountering. It was simple enough in the end. The property
stood between the mansions of two millionaires, Rothschild
and Stern, who, of their benevolence, were at that time providing
the municipality with the bulk of the funds required for the
relief of the city's poor. Whether bluntly or subtly, the city
government had been informed that if permission were given for
the hotel there would be no more money forthcoming for charity.

After two frustrating years of delay, an event happened which
changed Auzello's direction. Victor Rey had succeeded Elles as
managing director of the Ritz and he invited Auzello to return as
assistant manager. Auzello went to meet the board and intimated

that while he would like to come back to the Ritz he was prepared to do so only as manager. He was asked to leave the room. Ten minutes later he was recalled and offered the managership. The board was doubtful about the salary Auzello was asking, but he told them frankly that there were two kinds of hotel managers—those who were paid by the house and those who, in effect, paid themselves. He was in the former category. The board took his point and agreed to his terms.

So, in February 1925, Auzello returned to his first love, and the Ritz has been his life ever since. His hotel project fell through, but Auzello, the man of honour, eventually sold the property and paid out his backers. His own investment was lost.

*   *   *

The administrative heart of the Ritz is the small writing-room, near the Place Vendôme entrance, which M. Auzello converted into his office years ago by simply hanging a notice marked 'Private' on the curtained glass door. But the managing director has not the conventional executive love of sheltered privacy and as often as not the door stands open, for M. Auzello is susceptible to temperature and when he finds himself too warm he will kick the switch of the old-fashioned electric stove which stands behind a well-worn draught screen and open the door. Visitors who have lost their way often wander in, look a little bewildered and withdraw with a murmur of apology. Their surprise is understandable because the little room is not like any other in the hotel: it is bare-floored, homely, and frankly cluttered. (As has been already mentioned, it is dominated by a portrait of César Ritz.) Two plain glass-topped writing tables pushed together form Auzello's desk and there are stacks of folders, books and papers all around. The clear-desk convention is no use to an hotel man, he says; too many different things have to be within easy reach for quick reference.

Although the constant, wildly mixed flow of policy matters and the minutiae of hotel direction more than fill his working day, he likes to think and to talk about the wider issues of the business, and will give the switchboard orders to put no calls through to him for an hour while he enlarges on the subject closest to his heart.

He finds the French Government's attitude towards hotels infuriatingly contradictory: they want to boost tourism and at the same time, by taxation, they make running hotels difficult. He says that the hotel industry in France has never been considered by the Government as a serious and dignified economic business, and so has been consistently badly treated. If this attitude is not changed he thinks a great sector of the 'middle' hotel business is doomed. The extremes of frankly cheap hotels and the luxury hotels will survive, but the latter are having and will have a struggle to do so. Higher taxes than in any other industry and scarcity of labour are the main causes.

To illustrate the tax situation, Auzello asked the owners of two first-class hotels in Geneva and Zurich what their taxes amounted to and what the Ritz would have to pay if it operated in Switzerland. The answer was that in Geneva (which is in one of the most highly taxed cantons of Switzerland) the Ritz would pay 50 per cent less than it does and in Zurich 55 per cent less. When he told one of these boards what the Ritz paid at present, the chairman replied that if similar taxation were applied to his hotel all they could do would be to close the doors and go bankrupt. When foreigners compare holiday costs in France with Switzerland, usually remarking on how cheap, say, Geneva is and how expensive Paris is, they rarely take taxation into account.

Many Paris hotels, Auzello says, are 'going to pieces'. Often they have no more than a three-year lease and when the lease is renewed the rent always goes up. Hoteliers are therefore reluctant to spend money on improvements when they have such short certainty of tenure.

From the general to the particular, Auzello's favourite text is that while hotel-keeping *is* a business it cannot operate like any other; it has a sector which has to run with machine-like efficiency, but the most important part deals with people and no two people are alike. Every day brings problems which no machine can tackle. ('Where is the machine that can make a bed?') The task is to meet people's needs and wishes. Auzello says, 'We are in the business

of selling time under our roof to earn difficult money, and it
needs patience and psychology. Unlike other businesses, we cannot stock what is unsold and sell it the following day. An unlet
room is lost for ever.'

An hotel man can never know in advance what his next problem
will be or how he will deal with it. When the managing director
of the Ritz sits down at his desk at 8.30 any morning he is liable,
indeed almost certain, to find a wide variety of matters waiting
to be dealt with. One day when I was with M. Auzello his mail,
a fair sample, ranged over theft, insurance, tablecloths, menus,
stone-washing, furs, telephones and—this is a constant—the
individual requirements of future guests.

There had been a theft from one of the showcases in the long
gallery, which involved the police, and a check on the security
system of the hotel (which was, in fact, not at fault); this led to
the decision by M. Auzello that the insurance cover against such
contingencies should be increased.

A firm which has been making a particular linen tablecloth
(fifteen feet square) which the Ritz uses for the buffet and bar
tables at receptions had written to say that as the hotel was now
the only customer for this size of cloth it was no longer economic
to make them. This annoyed M. Auzello who, while he does not
set his face against change, likes to retain anything 'traditional'
to the Ritz, however small, when what is offered is not an im-
provement but a substitute.

Auzello's principle is to be prepared to make any change which
is practical and suitable, which will add to efficiency or comfort
without offending the taste of what he calls 'educated people',
who cherish the Ritz as it is. 'It must not damage the tradition,'
is how he puts it. But in the main he keeps to himself that he is
in the market for change at all, for one of the delicately sustained
illusions as between management and habitués is that nothing
ever changes at the Ritz. This means that (apart from the very
occasional major operation, like L'Espadon or the new bar)
Auzello has to make changes painlessly. His aim is to keep the
rooms 'in the tradition' but to slip in aids to comfort or con-
venience whenever it can be done unobtrusively.

When it is impossible to tell how guests will react to an innovation Auzello has been known to try practical experiments. For instance, the Ritz has always used only linen sheets and pillow-cases. César Ritz and his wife took infinite care over the choice of these when the hotel first opened and in Mme Ritz's lifetime there was never any question of making a change. But cotton sheets are far more general in the hotels of the world—and cotton sheets cost only half as much as linen. For the Ritz to go over to cotton would be an enormous saving, but would the customers notice or object?

Auzello bought enough cotton sheets to serve one floor on the Cambon side for a week. Immediately half-a-dozen guests asked, 'Why have you changed the sheets?' Auzello found they were not complaining about cotton as such; they were complaining about change, about something being different from what they were used to at the Ritz. The experiment ended abruptly.

Perhaps to take his mind off the irritating matter of the table-cloths, Auzello turned to a subject in which he had just had a small but satisfactory triumph. The general 'face-washing' of buildings which has given Paris a new and lovely bloom was in progress at this time and the Place Vendôme was spotted with honey-coloured buildings emerging, behind scaffolding and dust-sheets, from the mask of grime and soot which had long at least partially obscured their true beauty. The work on the Ritz had just been completed, but there had been a dramatic tussle behind the scenes.

A few days earlier Auzello's works manager had come to him and announced that an inspector from the Ministry of Beaux Arts (responsible to the Government for the execution of the law ordering the clean-up) had told him that work must stop immediately, as the cleaning was being done by the wrong method. M. Auzello had sent for the inspector and said that, while he was a law-abiding citizen and had the interests of the beauty of Paris (and especially the façade of the Ritz) as much at heart as any man living, he would like to know what the inspector's authority was for giving the stoppage order. The inspector replied that supervision of the work was vested in the Beaux Arts and he must control the methods used. He then specified the method required in place of the sand-and-water treatment being used. M. Auzello explained that he had gone into the matter thoroughly before the work was begun and satisfied himself that the sand-and-water method was suitable for the Ritz stone and that moreover the work could be done in this way in eleven days instead of the month or more other methods required. Bureaucracy moves slowly and the problem had resolved itself in Auzello's favour because the work went ahead and was finished on schedule. Whatever arguments might continue, the Ritz's face was washed —and very handsome it looked too.

Furs came into the managing director's agenda that morning because there was a letter from an old client making a reservation and M. Auzello remembered that the housekeeper had been taking care of this guest's wife's furs since her last visit, so these should now be brought out of store in readiness.

Telephones arose because two differently coloured models of the latest type of instrument had arrived and M. Auzello had to decide which the Ritz should have. This was a good example of change being accepted because it was functional (the new instruments were smaller, lighter and more attractive than the old black ones) and aesthetically sound. As though to prove he was no reactionary, M. Auzello tapped the black telephone beside him and said scornfully, 'This is for a museum.'

Letters from prospective guests all pass through M. Auzello's hands for the good reason that he has the longest memory in the hotel. A name that might not have any special significance for one of his younger subordinates may remind M. Auzello of some requirement—whim even—which, if anticipated, will enhance personal service for that guest. On such a letter he will scribble a quick note and pass it on for action.

There was, for instance, a letter from the secretary of an aged and ailing millionaire who occasionally stays at the Ritz. The managing director knew which suite he prefers, that he always dines promptly at seven o'clock and that he invariably has chicken. He also knew that this guest brings two personal servants, that the floor waiter must supply them in his pantry with the food they will serve but that he must not himself enter the suite. Breakfast would have to be ready at a punctual 6.45 a.m., which meant the floor waiter coming on duty fifteen minutes earlier than his usual time.

Letters making reservations provide an early source of information on which personal details of service can be organised; another is the duplicated list of the day's arrivals which is on Auzello's desk every morning—and also in the hands of thirty-five other key members of the Ritz staff. Compiling this (and the twin list of the day's departures) is a task of the night receptionist. For the managing director and his first assistant, the resident manager, it provides a reminder and summary of the day's movements; for others it serves a variety of purposes. It is the basis on which the housekeeper issues her orders to the chambermaids; it enables the *maîtres d'hôtel* to make favourite table reservations in anticipation of guests they are likely to be seeing later in the day.

M. Auzello moves swiftly through his work but he is wary of too much speed. The previous day he had been, as he said, 'pushed' into a buying decision by a younger executive. It was not a big matter, but he had the satisfaction that morning of having the younger man come in to acknowledge that he had made a mistake. M. Auzello admires his subordinate, so he smiled and shrugged, then said to me, 'He is very good, but he must learn that it is possible to go too quickly.'

Somewhere in the course of the day M. Auzello makes three excursions—to the kitchens, to the receiving point where the hotel provisions are delivered, and upstairs to the floors. His visit to the kitchens is always in the afternoon when things are quiet. There he has a conference with M. Lejour, the head chef.

This daily session is no mere ritual. Unlike many hotels which have a standing bill of fare in their restaurants, with a few *plats du jour* added, the Ritz has a new menu every day. M. Auzello says a little ruefully, 'We compile sixty menus a month where some people do one.' Two menu books are kept in the chef's headquarters, as one has to go to the girl who types and mimeographs every day sixty cards for lunch and forty for dinner. The books are important for reference in order to avoid repetition. If a diner sees a dish one day, and on his next visit, perhaps three weeks later, sees it again, he is apt to say, 'It's always the same old dishes here.' Memory can play tricks, and sometimes M. Auzello will say to Lejour, 'We had such-and-such a fortnight ago. We can't have it again so soon.' The chef may protest that it is at least two months since that dish was on, so the pages are turned back—and one or other proved to be right.

Whenever he can spare twenty minutes, M. Auzello visits the floors unannounced and checks that work in progress is going as planned. (He also makes various spot-checks, such as making sure that there is a *vase de nuit* in every bedside table and that it is scrupulously clean.) This habit is based on the military principle of the snap inspection. The key to proper control, says Auzello, is surprise.

Auzello is regarded by his staff as severe, which is attributed to his military background, but also extremely just and forgiving. He will speak sternly but never offensively, and the humbler the employee the more scrupulously polite he will be. He always wants to give a man another chance and the only limit he puts on his own forgiveness is when someone 'intentionally commits an act of open indiscipline or destruction'. He sums up his attitude to staff relations by saying: 'Usually a few convincing words will make a man return to doing his duty properly—and for ever.' He thinks it is 'a great responsibility to take away the bread from an employee's mouth when the man is simply ignorant'. Apart from the strike period in the Thirties, he estimates that he has not dismissed more than twenty people in nearly forty years.

One day, when Auzello had been expatiating to me on the problems of his job and his face was wearing a somewhat care-worn expression after a long day of the usual complex sort, he suddenly raised his hands, smiled and said in a different tone, to my surprise, 'It is amusing . . .' At that moment there was a knock on the door and a *concierge* came in and whispered something. Auzello's smile disappeared; his eyebrows and shoulders lifted and stayed there. I rose to go.

'Oh, no,' he said. 'It's nothing. Stay if you wish.'

A short, dark American of about forty was shown in. He smiled, but there was something set about his face that made me feel he had been working up determination about what he was going to do and say; a 'let's get this straight' expression if I ever saw one. The conversation that ensued would take too long to report, but the gist of it was this: a couple of months earlier the American had booked into the Ritz, by letter, for three days in Motor Show week, a time when all Paris is notoriously overcrowded. He had not arrived on the due day and the following day a letter of cancellation arrived. He was sent a bill and refused to pay it. The affair was still unsettled when he wrote again, announcing his imminent arrival in Paris and making a reservation. This had been refused. Now arrived and staying elsewhere, he had called on M. Auzello to have the matter out. His tone was a mixture of aggression and grievance.

M. Auzello listened patiently, but with a stern, slightly bored expression. At length he said, 'How would you like it if I ordered something from you, refused to pay for it, and then ordered something else?' The American looked surprised, hesitated, then said, 'I should take it badly.' 'So,' said M. Auzello, nodding sagely, 'you expect me to take it well?' He then explained very firmly why he was not prepared to receive the man as a guest again while the debt remained unpaid. There was nothing in this of the hotelier placating the awkward guest. It was a reprimand and a lecture on business ethics. At the end of it the American meekly said of course he would pay and that he would want to come to the Ritz again in the future. That, said M. Auzello, would be considered when it arose. The American nodded rather embarrassedly to me and left.

M. Auzello sighed. 'What I said!' he murmured. 'I would not take that from anybody. But he takes it. I have to do it.' He shrugged again and the closed-lips smile broadened. 'That's how things are nowadays.' Then, the incident dismissed, he returned to what he had been saying before the interruption. 'It's an amusing life,' he said, 'but you do not make much money.'

CHAPTER SIX

CRISIS IN THE CELLAR

WHEN VICTOR REY died in 1937 and Claude Auzello was appointed general manager of the Ritz, Hans Elmiger became his deputy with the title of manager, and remained so for seventeen years. He had been head of reception, first cashier, and for eleven years assistant manager.

Elmiger, a nephew of Hans Pfyffer, son of the discoverer of César Ritz, now runs the Hotel Grand National at Lucerne, which has long been in the Pfyffer family and with which César Ritz had close associations.

Having set his ambitions on an hotel career, Elmiger had a frustrating experience in the First World War when, at the age of nineteen, he was called up to the Swiss Army, then discharged because he suffered from asthma, but was thereafter not allowed to leave Switzerland while the war was on. As soon as peace brought him freedom of movement he lost no time and in the next six years he extended his experience by working in Naples, Cairo and—by the time he was twenty-seven—as manager of the Luxor Winter Palace.

He was back home in Lucerne in 1924 when his Uncle Hans telephoned urgently from Paris asking—or indeed ordering— him to come and help out at the Ritz, as Rey had had to fire six members of the reception and cashier departments in one day for dishonesty. Elmiger's mother tried to stop him going to Paris because he was in the midst of an asthma attack. He was determined, however, and during the journey he was several times near to collapse, but as he approached Paris, he has told me, he felt steadily better and has never had asthma since.

Already when he went to Paris Elmiger's hotel experience was considerable and his standards high, but he nevertheless was profoundly impressed by the Ritz. It was, he says, 'like a jewel-case—everything was perfect, no detail was overlooked and nothing left to hazard'. This was the legacy of César Ritz, and Elmiger says his own life as an hotel man has been based on what he has learned of Ritz. 'Discretion in all things was his watch-word, and it is mine,' he says.

*　　*　　*

Elmiger is remembered at the Ritz with the greatest respect and affection. A serious, thoughtful man, he has the air of a statesman or diplomat rather than an hotelier; like Auzello, there is nothing showy about him, no hint of the pompous or of switched-on charm, yet he has always been particularly successful in relations with guests and there is no doubt that he was a cherished friend rather than simply a superlative hotel manager to many Ritz regulars. One of my informants insisted that he was 'the most beloved' (it sounds fulsome in English, but it was patently sincere) manager the hotel has ever had.

But inevitably much of his Ritz career runs in parallel with that of Rey and, later and even more closely, Auzello. They lived through the same events and many of the same experiences. But Elmiger has to have a chapter to himself here, first because no account of the Ritz would be complete without him, but especially because of one story which is his alone.

During the German occupation, when the Ritz was mainly occupied by high-ranking German Army officers, Elmiger was responsible for most of the day-to-day dealings with them. He had the advantage that he was Swiss and German was his mother tongue. He determined to stay when others were leaving Paris in 1940 and just before the Germans arrived he held a meeting of the staff in the restaurant and told them that those who wanted to go were free to do so, especially the young men who might easily be sent to forced labour. The result was that when the Germans arrived the hotel staff had shrunk from 450 to eighteen.

The first order the Germans issued at the Ritz was that it should continue to be run as it always had been. Like Auzello, Elmiger was careful to be very 'correct' and avoided trouble with the Germans throughout the occupation. Looking back on it, he says that the German Foreign Service staff were much more difficult than the military and he also disliked the presence of the diplomats of Italy, Spain, and Japan who were allowed by the Germans to use the hotel. The Japanese particularly, he says, were 'very nasty'.

In the first months of the occupation the Germans kept strict control over French bank accounts and the only cash the Ritz management had was what the resident Germans paid for drinks. Their accommodation had to be paid for by the French authorities and the rate was twenty-five francs per day per room. (The franc was then about seventy to the pound.) This is the only time in its history when the Ritz lived a hand-to-mouth existence, simply using the little available money to buy what food could be had and to pay wages to the skeleton staff, with no thought of maintenance or profit. The good, if distinctly cold, relationship that Auzello and Elmiger maintained with the Germans saved the Ritz from the fate of many other hotels and requisitioned houses where the Germans either looted what they wanted or paid for it in worthless money.

The most memorable, and the most anxious, moment of Elmiger's war, indeed of his career, came in 1943 when the tide had turned against the Germans and they were taking every possible measure to hold down French resistance. They issued an order that all Frenchmen must immediately surrender weapons of any kind. Auzello very properly told the Germans that he could not answer or be held responsible for the contents of luggage stored with the Ritz. He was not prepared to open it or to guarantee that it did not contain any weapons.

A German sergeant and two soldiers were detailed to search the stored luggage and nothing was found. But Elmiger discovered that Auzello had also—and again properly—told the Germans that there was some more luggage stored in the Rue Lecourbe where the Ritz has its workshops and main cellars. Elmiger was horrified at the prospect of the Germans seeing the cellars with their magnificent stocks, then totalling about 120,000 bottles of wine. He felt sure they would be looted.

He drove out immediately to the Rue Lecourbe and told the soldiers he had come to supervise the searching of the luggage. He watched and waited anxiously, and at length the German sergeant suggested they should have something to drink. Elmiger contrived to get some wine up from the cellar without letting the Germans enter, but later they demanded more wine, and this time the sergeant followed Elmiger into the cellar. When the sergeant saw the vistas of wine on racks, Elmiger says, 'his eyes popped'.

As Elmiger had feared, the sergeant immediately made it clear that he regarded this as a wonderful treasure trove of loot. Elmiger knew they would simply bring up trucks and cart the wine away, and there would be nothing to be done about it. He was at his wits' end when he suddenly had a desperate idea. In his sternest, harshest German he said, 'You will not lay a finger on this wine. It is all the property of the Reichsmarschall.' He was gambling on the hope that they would never dare check on such a statement. Göring was staying at the Ritz at the time and the effect on the soldiers was electric. At the word 'Reichsmarschall' they came rigidly to attention, and the wine was never touched.

CHAPTER SEVEN
SON OF RITZ

CHARLES RITZ, chairman of the board of directors of the Ritz since 1953, the only surviving son of the founder and the only bearer of the name of Ritz now connected with the hotel, is a short, dapper, lively man of seventy-one, with crew-cut grey-black hair and a thin-line moustache; he looks, moves and thinks as though he were at least ten years younger. Although he is passionately—and that adverb is not too strong—interested in every aspect of the hotel he does not like to be thought of as an executive in the day-to-day sense (one reason why he does not have an office) and he will stress that he is not concerned with 'management', which he regards as the territory of M. Auzello, the managing director, whom he admires and treats with a mixture of veneration, protocol and affectionate bonhomie. It seems to be tacitly agreed between them that, although they are coevals, Charles Ritz is the 'modern' and Auzello the 'conservative'; this makes for a stimulating partnership. It is typical that M. Ritz would never dream of asking Auzello to come and see him, but, apart from the summer period when he goes fishing, he bounces into Auzello's office several times a day with some thought that is in the forefront of his wide-ranging and agile mind.

If M. Ritz has a definition of his function at the Ritz, aside from presiding at directors' meetings, it is as an ideas and details man. He feels that he can contribute most this way. The ideas are usually concerned with long-term policy and the details can be anything from personally designing an *hors d'œuvres* trolley which causes a minimum of disturbance as it is navigated among the tables to the precise tinting of the bulbs of the table-lights in the grill-room so that they will give the necessary illumination of the food while still flattering the feminine diner's *maquillage*.

He has an active sense of humour and refuses to take anything too seriously for long. He delights in making jokes at board meetings when he thinks their gravity excessive.

Charles Ritz would be the first to admit that he is a restless man. He has a horror of set routines, unlike his father who planned his days methodically. César could not bear *not* to have the time within sight. He would even have his watch on his desk or on his dressing table as he felt it was time-wasting to have to take it out and look at it. This explains why every room in the Ritz has a built-in clock. Charles Ritz says that his father, like all Swiss, had an obsession about time. Even the couriers' and private servants' rooms had clocks so that the occupants would have no excuse for being unpunctual for their employers. Charles Ritz has not inherited this Swiss characteristic from his father and is inclined to be indulgently mocking about it. 'Have you ever noticed,' he says, 'that if an aeroplane or a train is a minute late leaving or arriving it is always a Swiss who complains?'

For all his heritage of tact and diplomatic skill as an hotelier, Charles Ritz is constantly wary of the danger of being bored. 'I am not a drinking man,' he will tell you. 'I am not a party man. I am not a conversationalist. I can't force myself to listen to what doesn't interest me. I know this about myself, so I see as little as possible of the clientele.' He chuckles. 'I'm really a man of the woods, not of cities and society. But I have a passion for beauty. Ugliness or mediocrity—or chiselling on quality—is to me as a red rag to a bull. I cannot tolerate the second-rate. I don't think I'm extravagant, though I've probably inherited my father's impatience about the cost of what I know to be right. No, I go all out for the top in everything, but I always know what I can spend and keep within that.'

One day when I was in the office of the young secretary-general,

The Ritz facade at the opening in 1900. It was only six windows wide in those days.

César Ritz

(Studio René)

Facade of the Ritz (white awnings) in the Place Vendome. This was 1959 before the cleaning turned the Place to gold.

The interior garden — early morning.

The interior garden — gala dinner in 1930.

The visit of the Lord Mayor of London, June, 1939.

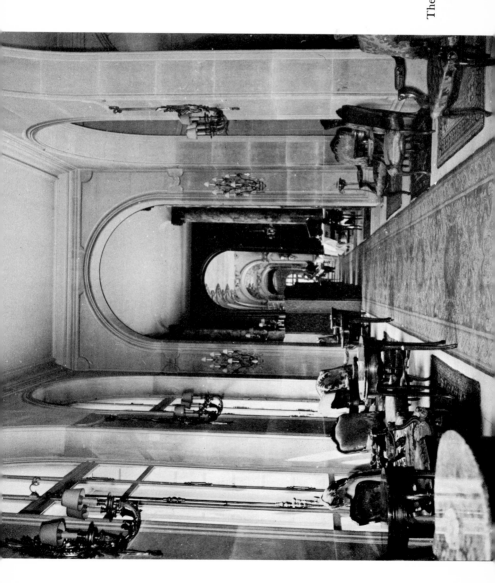

The entrance hall leading to the restaurant.

The restaurant at lunch time in 1962.

The Ritz bar — the most famous meeting place for the Haute Monde in Paris.

Entrance of the Ritz on Place Vendome, a Rolls Royce in foreground,

Bernard Penché, M. Ritz came to collect me. Penché had gone out of the room to look up some files for me and M. Ritz sat in the desk chair and swivelled around like a schoolboy for a moment. Penché came back into the room and M. Ritz leapt to his feet. Penché said, 'Please, don't disturb yourself.' But M. Charles scowled and said, 'To sit in that chair would drive me insane in a week.'

He hates being called 'Monsieur Ritz' or 'Monsieur le President' by the hotel staff; he has been known to say brusquely, 'There is only one president, *celui de la République.*' But, after years of trying, he cannot get the staff to call him 'Monsieur Charles', which is what he likes. One morning when he and I were going out together he went to fetch his overcoat from the Cambon cloakroom. The attendant was absent for the moment and on the solitary coat hanging on the pegs there was pinned a piece of paper with the words 'M. Ritz' written on it. If the man had been there probably nothing would have been said, for M. Ritz is invariably polite to the staff, most of whom he knows by name. But on this occasion he snatched the paper off and crumpled it with an angry growl which faded into a sigh as he murmured, 'Will they *never* learn?' Then he grinned at me. 'You know the real reason I don't like to hear my name used?' he said. 'If the guests hear it they may go for me. I don't want somebody with a grouch trying to put the blame on me.'

A little later, but still early, we went into the small bar on the Cambon side to talk. M. Ritz ordered his favourite Dutch lager and sampled the potato crisps which the bar-boys were setting out on the tables for the pre-lunch customers. Suddenly he called to Bertin, the barman, and switched into French. '*Exceptionelle,*' he said. '*Félicitations.*' He turned back to me (and to English) and, rubbing his fingertips together, said, 'Not a hint of grease on the fingers, yet they are very fresh.' Bertin acknowledged the compliment and added with a smile that the home-made crisps were always good. 'Oh, no,' said M. Ritz emphatically. 'They vary. Everything does. But today they are exceptional.' And he took up our conversation where he had left it.

M. Ritz makes no claim to be a gourmet—still less is he a

gourmand—but he insists that the important thing he inherited from his father was taste. He has, in fact, remarkably simple tastes. An Englishman who had known him for years took his wife to the Ritz for her first visit on their honeymoon. As they were about to enter the dining-room the husband said, 'If you see a man with a plate of spaghetti and a glass of beer, that'll be Charles Ritz.' The girl laughed, unbelieving. At the first table was just what her husband had foretold. M. Ritz jumped up to meet them and insisted on ordering for them a memorable lunch, with perfectly chosen wines.

Yet M. Ritz was what he describes as 'anti-grape' as a boy and did not drink spirits until he was sixty. His favourite foods are spaghetti and rice (with which he will probably have a delicate sauce of his own creation) and his idea of 'the perfect dish' is a piece of salmon, cut near the tail and poached with a champagne sauce containing mushrooms and fennel. Entertaining guests at dinner he will probably have a plain grilled chop and lager beer. He likes milk, especially sour, whisky (in small quantities) and he is greatly addicted to tea.

Lunching in a London club once, he glanced at the menu perfunctorily and then asked if he could have spaghetti and tea. The club had never had such an order before, but at an appealing glance from the host-member the head steward produced the spaghetti and a waitress appeared with a pot of tea, which, with hot water, milk, sugar and lemon, she placed rather doubtfully on a small side table at M. Ritz's elbow. M. Ritz was quite unaware of the surprise he produced—on the members as well as the staff.

With all food his first insistence is on the best raw materials and he is as dedicated as his father was to the 'eye-appeal' or presentation of food. He abominates people who 'mess up' food but he believes in what he calls 'ritzing it up', that is taking infinite pains about how it looks and how it is served. 'Let me watch food being served in a restaurant and have a look—just a look—in the kitchen,' he said, 'and I will tell you in five minutes if the place is any good, without having tasted anything.'

He has three basic rules about food: it must be hot; the raw materials must 'emerge'; and the dishes must look like what they are. 'One aims,' he said, 'not to fill the stomach so much as to stimulate the tooth.'

One evening in the grill-room, L'Espadon, which is his pride and joy, he sent back the toast which accompanied my caviare (he was having an unadorned grilled chop and drinking lager, though he chose my Meursault with loving care) because it was too thick. 'A poor man may want to spread his caviare thin and doesn't mind eating mainly bread,' he said. 'But *our* people want to taste caviare.'

One of the few differences in approach between the son and the father is that M. Charles does not believe, or even pretend to believe, that the customer is always right. He thinks even Ritz customers can sometimes be ridiculous and infuriating. He confesses to exasperation (concealed, of course) with people who order fastidiously and then become impatient awaiting the arrival of the dish. 'If it were served in the time they seem to think adequate,' he says, 'it would have to have been part-cooked in advance, and therefore ruined.' He is particularly critical of amateur experts, and even more so, if possible, of professional experts he regards as phoney—a word he frequently employs. There was an American restaurateur who arrived with an introduction to M. Ritz and was entertained by him in L'Espadon. The host ordered *foie gras* with the guest's full approval and then, says M. Ritz with ineffable disgust, 'he drank two Pernods'. After dinner the restaurant man asked if he might prepare a dish. M. Ritz took him to the kitchen. He chose two *Manche* (Dover) soles, filleted them and put them in pickle for the next day. For his host this just about summed up the man's rating in the world of *cuisine*.

When he goes to one of the bars, he enjoys the fact that he can sit happily incognito so far as ninety per cent of the customers are concerned and is quite prepared to eavesdrop when they talk about the hotel. He will sip a whisky before dinner, and while a guest will not forfeit his friendship by having a dry martini he can be caustic about what he calls the 'cocktail approach' to the main event of the evening, which is dinner. However important the revenue of the bars may be to the hotel, M. Ritz still thinks the cocktail habit deplorable. Of private or amateur cocktail-making he says contemptuously, 'They put in everything, including gunpowder, and if they survive it's a great success.'

* * *

Charles Ritz went to America in 1916—having been discharged by the Swiss Army—because of an offer from Frank Munsey, the newspaper publisher, who had hotel interests and wanted somebody to help run his Mohican Hotel at New London, Connecticut. With his European ideas of what was correct, young Ritz reported for duty in a swallow-tailed coat and was immediately told by the manager, 'This is an hotel, my boy, not an undertaker's parlour.'

In his early days in America, M. Ritz worked for a time at the Ritz-Carlton in New York, which operated under licence from the Paris Ritz. He describes this period as 'non-creative'. 'I was set to watch the waiters and see they didn't break too many plates,' he says. 'My other job was "minding the store" in the evening while the managers went out.' Having nothing to do he took to buying second-hand fishing rods, often from pawn-brokers, taking them to pieces and remaking them according to his own ideas. He then sold them to guests who were interested, and eventually even to a sports emporium on Fifth Avenue. This hobby not only showed a profit but began his career as a designer of fishing rods; he is still adviser and consultant to the largest firm of fishing-tackle makers in Europe.

Early in 1918, at the age of twenty-seven, he joined the American Army and became a sergeant in a unit concerned with morale. He spoke English, French, German and Italian fluently and was assigned to interview and report on immigrant soldiers who, by reason of their enlistment, were entitled to U.S. citizenship if they were thought suitable. He also at this time himself acquired American citizenship and remained a dual Swiss-American national for many years.

When the war was over M. Ritz began a period of widely varied enterprises, none of them connected with the hotel business but all of them providing him with an active and somewhat adventurous business life. In New York he met Claude Rochefort, grandson of a famous French journalist, Henri Rochefort. Claude was an engineer by profession but both he and Charles Ritz were keen fishermen and they were more concerned with going fishing in Maine than with their careers. The trouble was they also had to make money. Charles had the idea that they could combine business and pleasure by showing films to holiday-makers. They clubbed together to buy a 150-dollar projector, hired a print of *The Birth of a Nation* and set themselves up in business at Poland Springs. Rochefort turned the projector handle and Charles was the cashier. The commercial basis of the enterprise was that on 50 dollars film hire they could hope to take 200 dollars in admissions. It didn't occur to them to run the film through before the first show with the result that it broke down fourteen times and the performance finished at one a.m. However the audience took it in good part and didn't leave, and thereafter the business went ahead prosperously.

The following summer they set up another movie house at Ormond Beach, Florida. John D. Rockefeller was staying there and Ritz, always the ideas man, hired an operator to photograph the old man, who had never been filmed before.

With another partner, a Hungarian, Ritz formed the Ritz Motion Picture Corporation of America and found a new location at Spring Lake, New Jersey. Here they bought a small theatre which a local barber had been running and out of which he had made enough money to retire. With pride Charles put up the first 'Ritz' sign over a cinema. For local attraction he shot film on the beach in the morning and invited the holiday-makers to come along in the evening and see themselves. Once a month he varied the film shows with prize fights. Around 1920 he introduced the first curved cinema screen and later he operated two Ritz cinemas at Long Beach.

His next venture was entirely different. He found that a friend in France was making musical boxes, in various forms such as powder-boxes and whisky-jugs, and obtained the agency for these in the United States. For this purpose he formed the Ritz Import and Export Corporation, with a tiny office just off Times Square.

One of the main attractions of this office, he recalls, is that it looked out on the theatre where the Ziegfeld Follies were playing and Ritz spent many happy hours in summer watching the beauties cooling themselves on the fire-escape. Unfortunately he had to interrupt this enjoyable practice, as his goods had to be sold, and, laden with three large trunks, he worked a strenuous itinerary giving shows of his wares in hotels all over America.

He enjoyed America so much that he had no thought of returning to Europe and when his mother insisted in 1928 that it was time for him to come back to Paris he says, 'It nearly broke my heart'. In Paris he did not immediately go to work in the hotel. He saw no suitable role for himself at the Ritz at that time. His restless versatility soon found employment and he became a customer's man for a New York brokerage firm. Then, to help one of his clients, he undertook to run a shoe-shop which was badly in need of new ideas. Here again Ritz was able to be creative. When he told me that his shop was the first in Paris to put scenery into the windows I was not sure what he meant. But thirty-five years ago window display tended to be a functional business of simply putting the merchandise on show; what Charles Ritz did was to introduce décor in the theatrical sense— for instance, creating appropriate settings for seasonal goods.

His inventiveness brought about one major and lasting innovation in footwear. In Murren one winter he saw women dancing in their ski-boots and thought it hideous. Back in Paris he saw Charles Creed, the couturier, at Weber's one day wearing a short boot (or high shoe) much favoured by British Army officers. Ritz adapted this in two-tone suede and leather for women, and so the *après-ski* boot, suitable for wearing with trousers, was born. He also designed a gold sandal which was, as he says, 'pretty, cheap and comfortable'. Its inexpensiveness derived from the fact that it consisted largely of two straps which were made of lampwick and gilded.

During the Second World War he had more leisure than he liked and it was then that he tackled a project he had long thought about but for which he had never found time—the writing of a book about fishing. He had felt for years that there were far too many sacrosanct ideas in fly-fishing and he thought it was time somebody exploded the myths and produced a book which was at once expert, based on experience, practical and revolutionary. The book, *A Fly Fisher's Life*, with an introduction by the late Ernest Hemingway, now sells steadily in English, American, French and German editions.

L. de Boisset, one of France's most famous writers on fly-fishing, says of Charles Ritz, in his foreword to the French edition, 'He has been wonderfully successful in reconciling his duties as director of the greatest hotel in the world with the demands of his sport'.

De Boisset also tells how, after years of study and experiment, Ritz in 1939 'set up a laboratory in the Faubourg Saint-Honoré, the street in which elegance and taste triumph. There was a façade to his piscatorial lair: a high-class shoe-shop of which Charles Ritz was director. But it was only a façade. The real interest lay elsewhere, in a vast room behind the shop.

'Every evening, the initiated met there at about six o'clock. By-passing the shop, you went in the back way, pushing open a door, to the right of which the delightful Pierre Creusevaut was to be found assiduously crouched over a ledger with innumerable columns. This was also part of the façade. Having passed the time of day with him, you entered the sanctuary where the daemon-possessed Ritz welcomed his visitors amid an unlikely collection of rod-tips, whole and split bamboos, vices, files, glue pots, lines of all varieties and sizes, plain and automatic reels, pliers, callipers, and other instruments of precision.

'It was here, within these walls, whose empty spaces were decorated with superb fishing photographs, that the master explained to his attentive disciples the reasoning behind the theories and the results of his experiments. When the lease fell in and the god of commerce expelled the daemon of fishing from his citadel, all the fly-fishermen of Paris went into mourning.'

The Pierre Creusevaut mentioned above was one of the most important figures of this exclusive meeting-place. He was for many years the world's champion professional fly-caster. Charles Ritz employed him as accountant of the shoe-shop so that he could have him with him in the fishing-room as much as possible.

But even if his 'citadel' has gone now, Charles Ritz maintains not only his passionate interest in the technicalities of fly-fishing but his pleasure—a need, perhaps, to talk fishing with fellow-practitioners or to instruct the less expert.

Every year he gives a fly-fishermen's dinner party at the Ritz, which may be attended by thirty or forty carefully chosen guests from all over the world. (This is the annual dinner of Ritz's own private club—the International Fario Club—and membership is restricted to his personal fishing friends. In fact the annual dinner is the club's only function and purpose.) It is not unknown for guests to fly from America for this one evening. There is one firm rule, however: an invited guest who declines, without what Ritz regards as a good and sufficient reason, is never asked again.

He will also, at the expense of seemingly more important engagements, fly to England and spend two strenuous days at a sportsmen's convention or agricultural show giving demonstrations of casting and free tuition and advice to anybody who seems seriously interested in the art of what he will often call, with a curious and revealing absence of sporting euphemism, 'killing fish'.

* * *

A man who has reached his seventies, steeped all his life in the traditions of a great hotel and *haute cuisine*, could hardly be blamed if he were inclined to live in the past, deploring modern trends and sighing for the 'great days' when every dinner party was a banquet. But Charles Ritz maintains that his real interest is in the future; the past is important only for preservation of what he calls 'the indisputable traditions'. Far from wanting to see his customers eat as their fathers and grandfathers did, he believes there are inescapable reasons for the changes in taste. People used to eat more, he says, because they had more leisure, they took more exercise and the air was purer. He is sure that the motor-car, 'loading the air with carbon monoxide', is responsible for diminished appetites. 'Also,' he says, 'rooms are nearly always overheated nowadays.'

As people have become more and more diet-conscious, he argues, they have turned to simpler dishes, more simply cooked. This explains the greatly increased demand (which he has encouraged) for grilled meat and for sea-food—and why these are the specialities of his grill-room. The rich sauces of the old days are not wanted with this kind of food (nor are the heavier wines), so all the sauces are now made much lighter than they used to be. But they are still very important; it is the sauce, says M. Ritz, which sells the fish.

He has always had a particular interest in sauces. There is one popular sauce at the Ritz which he invented almost by accident many years ago. In those days he often fished in Canada, both on the Atlantic coast and the Pacific. Salmon, trout and black bass were the principal catches. He and his companions camped out on those trips and because of his background the others would insist that Ritz should take care of the catering and cooking. Their basic food, of course, was fish and after a while it became monotonous and he decided something would have to be done to give it a new flavour.

There was always among their provisions some English mustard—'you know, that lovely-looking powder in a little can with some yellow paper round it'. Normally, for salmon, *hollandaise* is used when the fish is eaten hot and *mayonnaise* for cold salmon. These sauces were impossible in the circumstances, so Ritz mixed up the English mustard with cream and butter. The result was a very light *mousseline* sauce, and they all liked it very much. The reason was simple: with a fish which has a good deal of natural fat an oily sauce is inclined to be too rich. When chefs make a *sauce moutarde* they use *hollandaise*, which Ritz thinks too heavy.

When he went back to Paris after one of those trips he decided to try out the sauce at the hotel. He explained the recipe to the chef and *sauce Mousseline moutarde* with fish has been a great success ever since. The same sauce, incidentally, with a few herbs added, can be treated as *sauce verte* and put in the refrigerator to be used cold instead of mayonnaise.

The Ritz creed, in essence, is that to make any sauce you need butter and cream, and basically the success of a sauce depends on them. After travelling widely around the world M. Ritz is convinced that only in France are sauces to be found as they should be. The reason is that France has Normandy cream.

Normandy cream starts like any other cream—by skimming the milk. But in America, for instance, it is usually put in the ice-box and afterwards it is, in Charles Ritz's words, 'homogenised, pasteurised, whatever you call it'. In Normandy, the peasant does not get enough cream in one day to be able to sell it. He has no ice-box, so he puts it in a large jar in his cellar and keeps on adding to it every day until Friday comes. By that time he has a cream which has turned slightly sour, which is a little thick— *la crème double*. This is the ideal cream for making sauces.

The next thing is the butter. Sweet butter is not right; salt butter is not good; it must be absolutely natural butter, not too sweet. 'In Normandy,' says M. Ritz, 'they leave the cows out in the fields and let them take care of themselves. They graze on soil which has no artificial fertiliser and they have no artificial food. In America, the cream and the butter—the cream especially— are too sweet because the cattle are not kept and fed in this way. Besides their natural food, they are given corn and even sometimes molasses and other types of artificial food to obtain quick fattening and the famous American "steak cuts". Unless you have absolutely natural cream and butter you cannot make good sauces. The moment you try to thicken a sauce with flour it is dead.'

* * *

I have spent many hours with Charles Ritz and whatever effect I may have had on him he has never come within miles of boring me. Indeed boredom is so much his *bête noire* that he will often tell a story so fast or so condensed that one has to ask for expansion to get its full value. He would much rather be off on another subject. It is impossible not to be entertained by a man whose conversation ranges—darts, rather—over more than half a century, goes swiftly from country to country, from theories and generalisations based on hard experience to sharp anecdotes which can swiftly sum up one of the thousands of personalities he has known.

He can go in a flash from the serious to the richly comic; suddenly confessing that as a good Swiss he often yodels when he lands a fish, then telling of his pet magpie, Maggie, whom he transported from the South of France to Paris during the war, stopping to fish for its food en route. He will suddenly interrupt himself to ask you to send him from London a particular catalogue of model railways ('H–O track, Marklin, three-rail system') and then look astonished when you don't know what he is talking about. (If you are favoured, he will show you the room at the top of the hotel which is entirely taken up with his model railway system, the most elaborate and ingenious I have ever seen. He took up this hobby only a couple of years ago.)

He likes to produce even the most fleeting shock in his listener. 'Have I ever told you how I went to bed with Sarah Bernhardt?' he will say and watch for the effect. Then he will explain that when he was a small boy, and his father was running the Savoy in London, Bernhardt was a regular visitor and a friend of the family. Loving children, she liked the little boy to come to her room in the morning and climb into her bed. Another child-loving friend of those far-off days was the Grand Duke Nicholas of Russia. Although when he came to Paris he lived in formidable style in the Ritz's royal suite (M. Ritz remembers vividly that the doors were always guarded by giant Cossacks), he missed his children and Charles used to be summoned to be dandled on the royal knee and to play humpty-dumpty.

Even his manner of talking—fluent, idiomatic English which has both a French and an American accent, or French with a sprinkling of Americanisms—has its own stimulation, but the speed and variety of what he has to say rivet attention.

While he was talking to me about cream and butter, he suddenly, though logically enough, switched to cheese and then demanded, 'Why is there no good French cracker?' According to M. Ritz, the only accompaniment worthy of a good cheese is a particular thin water biscuit made in England. 'American saltines are okay,' he said grudgingly, 'but that English biscuit is ideal.

I wonder why we can't make them here.' One had the feeling he might jump out of his chair and go down to the kitchen and try his hand at biscuit-making. The reason why the Ritz company has a tie-up with Ritz crackers, incidentally, is not basically commercial; M. Ritz simply thinks they are first-class biscuits. He then informed me that there were only two marmalades worth eating—one orange and the other lime, both ordinary branded articles you can buy in any British grocer's.

We were at lunch at this time and suddenly I noticed that my host's eyes were roving and I knew something was irritating him. He does not drink coffee after meals but he had noticed before we had that my wife's cup and mine had been empty for a few moments without a waiter offering to refill them. He muttered something I didn't catch and I asked him to repeat it. 'Table radar,' he said. 'That's what a good waiter has. He needn't be hovering near you all the time; he just knows when something is required. He answers before you call. No restaurant has more than one or two real radar waiters. Some of the rest seem to wear ear-flaps when you want them.' (Curiously enough, a *chef de rang*—or captain—named Contamine, who has been at the Ritz since 1925 and is regarded as a model waiter, is stone-deaf; but nothing escapes his eye.)

Charles Ritz went on with the subject of waiters. 'You know one of the big troubles with waiters?' he said. 'Business men having business lunches. The sort of men who are only in first-class restaurants because of business, impressing their clients on the expense account. Frankly, they are not up to it. They are not connoisseurs and their attention is not on their food. The waiters know this, so they are not on their toes. Once a waiter has got away with slackness the trouble is he may become slack with people who *do* know. You have to watch carefully or they get slack'—he chuckled at his own coming joke—'or come to work in slacks.' I laughed. 'I mean it,' he said. 'Slacks—all colours, if you don't stop them. Miami shirts too.

'I sometimes put it to waiters this way: a customer may look all right, but he may be going to throw a hand grenade and a good waiter must be ready to catch it before it hits the ground.'

The talk turned to that important, pervasive word in the vocabulary of hoteliers—discretion. 'You must know how to deal with anything—including the impossible,' he said. 'There is no situation that cannot be handled without offending the customer. For example, Galopin (who runs the theatre-ticket stand in the Ritz lobby) once gave me a very good example of what I mean. Three men came up to him one evening and one of them said, "We want three girls." What was Galopin to do? Put his nose in the air and say, "We do not do that sort of thing at the Ritz"? No. Procure girls? Worse. Galopin said, "You want three seats for the Folies Bergère?" and sold them just that.

'Discretion means many things. Not overdoing anything, for example. You know we like our staff, especially on the floors, to know the clients, to remember their likes and dislikes and so on—in fact to make them feel at home. But one housekeeper, years ago, had a favourite client and when she knew this guest was arriving she went and met the boat-train with a bouquet of flowers. She had to be fired.'

Any dismissal makes M. Ritz a little sad. But no one at the Ritz is ever fired unless it has become inevitable. One case particularly worried him, but there was no other solution. During the Second World War there was a chef who, in the midst of desperate shortages of raw materials, performed miracles of ingenuity.

'He produced varied dishes with varying names which were basically a little chicken, a little veal and a little rabbit,' M. Ritz recalls. 'He used to go and sit in the Tuileries Gardens brooding over whether to make it *blanquette de veau* or *poulet* something. But when the war was over and things were becoming easier we realised he was finding it difficult to adjust to having proper supplies. We had to stop him from being over-economical. In the end he had to go.' He quickly added, 'He was near retiring age anyhow, so it was no hardship. We just couldn't stand the strain of keeping an eye on him. Imagine having a Ritz chef who is stingy with materials!'

Sometimes the hotel man has to put his foot down very firmly with guests, but there is always a way to do it. Charles Ritz told

[135]

me that Olivier once flatly refused to have a dish prepared as a woman wanted it for a dinner party she was arranging. She wanted roast turkey stuffed with oysters. 'Olivier talked her out of it,' said M. Ritz, 'and I think she was rather ashamed of having had such a barbaric idea.'

On one occasion, talking of Jean Pascaud, who designed the Ritz Bar in 1936 and the new Vendôme cocktail lounge in 1962, M. Ritz said, 'He has young ideas. He likes cha-cha-cha.' Charles Ritz too has young ideas. He thinks, for example, that it is possible when redecorating Ritz rooms to make them gay without spoiling their traditional style. He wants to eliminate French grey paint ('too cold') and replace it with a particular pale blue. He thinks guests will feel the difference rather than notice it. He has an overall scheme for Ritz redecorations based on three colours—which he calls *champagne rosé*, *champagne blanc*, and *azur*. The Ritz workshops make all the hotel's paints and, if necessary, for some special job he has dreamed up M. Ritz will personally supervise the mixing until he has got exactly the shade he wants.

*   *   *

The national or, to use a dangerous word, racial characteristics of hotel guests are not a subject on which hoteliers are apt to be very forthcoming. This is perhaps partly natural discretion and partly because experience shows that there is good and bad in all nationalities and it is both unfair and unsafe to generalise too widely. Charles Ritz, however, was prepared to tackle this question when I asked him to, at least in relation to eating habits and tastes. He offered me some racy, off-the-cuff comments, but later, having given the matter more thought, he produced for me a typewritten memorandum which he had dictated. It was in French and, while it would be easy enough to summarise and paraphrase it, the original, even in my dubious translation, seems to justify quotation in full as it also offers a sidelight on M. Ritz's sharply perceptive style:

'If you find pieces of bread on the chairs when clearing the tables you can be practically certain that the customers have been

French. The French customers are certainly the most difficult and often nasty in petty ways.

'The Belgians are the biggest eaters (*très gourmands*)—difficult, fussy about details, and they always eat potatoes. But they are excellent customers and always tell you when they like things.

'The Norwegians eat a little bread in place of potatoes; they drink a lot and are not connoisseurs.

'Only the English know about game and how and when to eat it.

'The Americans drink too many cocktails in the bar, which often makes them drink minerals during the meal and that does not help the palate. There are, however, a number of Americans who have lived for a long time in Paris and have become great connoisseurs—of wine above all. In general they win the confidence of the *maître d'hôtel*.

'The Italians and the Spanish are very hard to please. They all have their own particular ideas and do not put their faith in the *maître d'hôtel*.

'Before the war the best customers were the Russians and the Germans, but only the Russians were connoisseurs.

'The English are almost as much connoisseurs of food and cooking as the French. Thanks perhaps to the work of Ritz and Escoffier in London during the *belle époque*, they are educated.

'In general, the customer who sits down at the table determined to show his convivial friends that he knows everything, describes the menu to them and tries to show the *maître d'hôtel* that he knows more than he does, is often a person living in Paris who, finding himself with foreign visitors, feels he has to show off. He is the worst critic of all.

'The good customer is the man who is perfectly educated in food and wine and knows at once whether or not the *maître d'hôtel* is someone in whom he can place his confidence.

'The restaurateur who has the British, Belgians, Germans and French business men for his clients always makes big profits.'

*   *   *

[137]

One evening when I had arranged to meet Charles Ritz before going out to dinner he bustled in a few minutes late and gave, quite unself-consciously, a perfect demonstration of his kaleidoscopic approach to life and conversation. He had been standing out in the Place Vendôme, he said, watching a young man tinkering with his sports car. It was an up-to-the-minute model Jaguar and the young man was at once obviously distressed that something was wrong with it and also unwilling to admit his technical ignorance. He had the bonnet up and was flicking here and there uncertainly with a spanner. A gendarme on the beat was offering half-hearted advice and a little non-strenuous assistance.

What made M. Ritz chuckle about this was that the young man was the former King Peter of Jugoslavia, on his way to dine at L'Espadon. His father, King Alexander, was a regular Ritz patron for many years. Somehow for Charles Ritz, this vignette summed up the same-yet-changing aspect of the Ritz: royalty still came, but instead of having the carriages and the entourage they came alone, drove themselves and had to fix their own cars when they broke down.

He told this story more quickly, I suspect, than I have done and the next moment he was remembering that he needed a replenishment of cigars from Dunhill's of London and would I bring them the next time I came to Paris? Then, switching to the dinner I was going off to and insisting again that he does not regard himself as gourmet or connoisseur, he recommended a sauce I might easily not have thought of, and as we parted he suddenly and thoughtfully delivered himself of something which contains the material of an epitaph for himself as hotelier. 'I know about details,' he said, 'and if I have introduced or perfected a hundred details in my time I shall be content. After all, no chef has ever invented a hundred dishes.'

CHAPTER EIGHT

THE RITZ BARS

'Good morning, Mister, Sir or Count,
What will it be today?'
And Frank awaits the deft reply:
'The same as yesterday.'
Ode to the Ritz Bar,
J. Ainsworth Th. Morgan, 1921

THE OTHER twenty-four lines of Mr Morgan's amiable ode are rather worse doggerel, but the point is that few bars have odes written and published about them at all. The 'Frank' who for the poet personified the Ritz Bar was Frank Meier, the head barman from the opening of the hotel's first bar in 1921 until he died in 1947.

He was, by general consent, the reason for the Ritz Bar becoming the best-known in Paris, both because he was a great expert (his book, *The Artistry of Mixing Drinks*, is still regarded as the definitive work) and because of his personality. His customers became his friends—ranging from President Theodore Roosevelt, who insisted on Frank sitting at his table when they crossed the Atlantic together once, to Porfiro Rubirosa, who enjoyed the privilege of dining regularly at Frank's home.

Frank set the style of the barman whose function is largely social, who circulates and greets people, hears their confidences, solves their problems, fixes things generally; he even played

[139]

backgammon with them. It became a personal favour if Frank went behind the bar and mixed your drink himself.

His successor, the present head barman, George Scheuer, was a thirteen-year-old pageboy when the bar opened but he swiftly became Frank's disciple and lieutenant, so now, while still in his fifties, he has an association with the bar going back forty-two years, interrupted only by his war service.

There are now three Ritz bars, all under George's supervision, but it is the largest of these, on the left just inside the Rue Cambon entrance of the hotel, which is known throughout the world as 'the Ritz Bar', which that old Paris hand, Art Buchwald, has described as 'one of the oldest and most famous drinking institutions in France'. It is there that George is usually to be found. Like Frank, he is rarely seen behind the bar, his preference being to perambulate, talk to his friends and ensure that all is going smoothly. With his always immaculate white coat, his pink cheeks and his beaming smile, George follows in the Frank tradition of being a host rather than a barman, but there is nothing grand about his playing this role, which really amounts to being an international character; he will empty an ashtray, clear away glasses, or take an order as readily as any of his staff, at least one of whom, Michel, is in fact his senior in years and service at the Ritz.

*   *   *

The original bar was across the end of the room, a massive mahogany affair—like an English bar, some people will tell you, but Frank's son, Jean-Jacques, has a small-boy memory of it as being like the western saloon of the movies, complete with spittoons. (These were discarded when it was found that nobody at the Ritz spat and the cuspidors were merely used as receptacles for cigar and cigarette butts.) There was a screen across the entrance, and if a woman was unwise enough to enter—or put her head in to look for her husband—the custom, however deplorable, was for the men to start up a concert of whistles and continue it until she retreated.

But with time and emancipation the encroachment of women could not be withstood. Across the lobby there was a small, panelled writing-room. It became the custom for ladies to wait there for their menfolk to emerge from the bar. Gradually it had to be faced that the ladies too might like a drink. So one of the bar waiters, Bertin, was assigned the job of taking the feminine orders and carrying the drinks over. At this point men were not allowed in the writing-room alone, but they *could* join their ladies there. Soon the little room became overcrowded. In fact what the Ritz was having to accept was that men and women in the new, freer world liked to have their drinks together.

So, in 1936, the main bar was remodelled and thrown open to both sexes. But the former writing-room now had its own clientele, so it was transformed into a bar too, and, managed by Bertin, it functions independently.

* * *

Many students of bar philosophy regarded Frank Meier as the perfect barman and one of his friends and regular customers, Prince de Viggiano, who wrote the foreword to *The Artistry of Mixing Drinks*, summarised the requirements which Frank fulfilled. A 'true mixologist', he said, was something of a chemist and a psychologist; he must 'develop some of the qualities of the chameleon, yet retain a personality of his own'.

Frank obviously titled his book with care: 'artistry' was to him an essential of cocktail-making. 'The cocktail should always be perfect', he wrote. 'There is no reason ever to drink a bad one. Almost any of the ingredients of which cocktails are composed might better be consumed "straight" rather than just carelessly poured together.'

He had no false modesty or lack of faith in his own recipes. Use only the best ingredients, mix with infinite care and, he declared, 'the result will be the Miracle-Cocktail which has made the Ritz Bar famous'.

Frank even had a special message for the younger generation. He wanted to be sure that they understood what might be called the facts of bar life. 'The art of rational drinking', he wrote, 'is an accomplishment as indispensable as dancing or bridge, and a fair knowledge of wines and liqueurs, their provenance, characteristics, best years, etc., forms part of a gentleman's culture. Any young man who can convince me that his lips will never touch alcohol need not follow my required course in drinks and drinking. To know how to drink is as essential as to know how to swim, and one should be at home in both these closely related elements. Each man reacts differently to alcohol; he should know before the time when, according to custom, he indulges in his first collegiate "binge", whether liquor affects his head, his legs or his morals; whether he sings, fights, weeps, climbs lamp-posts or behaves with excessive affection toward the opposite sex; whether, in short, it makes him a jovial companion or a social pest. "*In vino veritas*" does not mean that a man will tell the truth when in drink, but he will reveal the hidden side of his character.'

Frank's version of how the cocktail got its name neatly combines his French domicile and his American clientele. He does not vouch for the story's authenticity and says that perhaps 'the inventor of this boon to mankind will always remain unknown'.

The story he tells is of Betsy Flanagan who in 1779 ran a tavern near Yorktown where the American and French officers of the Revolutionary Army used to meet and drink. A neighbour of Betsy's, an Englishman with whom Betsy was in a state of permanent feud, kept poultry, and Betsy was always threatening to raid his coops and give her Revolutionary customers a chicken dinner at the expense of the enemy. They teased her about the delay in serving this feast until one night Betsy invited them into the dining-room and there was the chicken dinner.

In the bar afterwards Betsy proudly exhibited the feathers of the chickens. Betsy already had a concoction which was popular with the officers but had no name other than a 'bracer'. Celebrating their hostess's banquet amid the cock feathers, the officers toasted her—and the colonists' cause—in bracers. One officer brandished a bracer and shouted, '*Vive le* cocktail'. Frank ends his story, somewhat lamely, with 'The name stuck'.

Whatever the authenticity of Frank's legend, there seems to be no doubt that the cocktail had its origins in America, and that, contrary to a popular belief that it was a product of the 1920s, it is more than a century older.

It was defined in 1806 as 'a stimulating liquor, composed of spirits of any kind, sugar-water and bitters' and in 1809 Washington Irving wrote in his *Knickerbocker's History of New York* that the natives 'lay claim to being the first inventors of those recondite beverages—cock-tail, stone-fence and sherry-cobbler'.

Frank lists six other cobblers—brandy, champagne, claret, port, Rhine wine and Sauternes. The trend of taste away from sweet drinks towards dry is probably responsible for the fading of the cobbler; the sherry variety, for instance, consists of a tumbler two-thirds full of cracked ice into which is poured a teaspoonful each of sugar and orange juice and which is then filled up with sweet sherry, stirred and served 'decorated with the fruit of season'.

Another theory about the origin of 'cocktail' is less picturesque than Frank's, but it is based on a process of transference common in the history of words. One name for a horse that is not quite a thoroughbred is a 'cocktail' and hence (as the Oxford Dictionary confirms) the word came to be applied to humans, to describe someone who 'passes for a gentleman but is in fact not of gentle breeding'.

Frank's book is now something of a collector's item; published in 1936 in three limited editions—the first of only twenty-six copies, especially for the author—it has long been out of print and in many ways it is a fascinating period piece. In less than 200 pages it covers a remarkable amount of ground in addition to the cocktail recipes, but the main, or alcoholic lore section, is itself encyclopaedic, if at times a little mystifying even to someone who was a reasonably sophisticated frequenter of bars a quarter of a century ago.

After listing some 300 cocktails and mixed drinks Frank goes on to fifty pages divided into sections devoted alphabetically to such categories of other drinks as Cobblers, Coolers, Crustas, Daisies, Egg Nogs, Fixes, Fizzes, Flips, Highballs, Juleps, Punches, Rickeys, Sangarees, Scaffas, Shrubs, Slings, Smashes, Sours, Toddies and Zooms.

What, you may well ask, is or was a Daisy?—or a Smash?— or a Zoom? Frank offers no definition of a Daisy *per se*, but a good example is his Morning Glory Daisy in which are shaken up half a white of egg, the juice of half a lemon, a little sugar, two teaspoonfuls of Pernod and brandy (or gin or rum or whisky as preferred) with a dash of soda water added.

A Smash is defined as a miniature julep, based on gin, rum or whisky. An example of the species Zoom is the Bacardi Zoom, which Frank invented for the Comte Jean de Limur. (Many of his original recipes are dedicated to individuals for whom they were created.) A teaspoonful of honey is dissolved in a little boiling water, then poured into a shaker to which are added a teaspoonful of fresh cream and the rum, and the result is strained into a wine-glass.

The change in drinking tastes between the Twenties and the Sixties amounts to a minor social revolution. It is not so much that what is popularly drunk is totally different; it is that the range of popular drinks has diminished so greatly. In the early Thirties the cocktail was at its peak, and the variety offered was bewildering. Now, on the evidence of one's own eyes and ears plus the confirmation of George, the great majority of drinks served in the Ritz Bar are whisky, champagne (straight or in cocktail) and dry martinis, made with gin or vodka. Vodka crops up again in the occasional—usually matutinal—Bloody Mary, ordered by Ritz waiters from the barman as '*un bloody*', pronounced as though 'blood' rhymed with 'rude'.

Frank's heyday was also the heyday of the cocktail, and the change in tastes is what gives his book its charming period flavour. Names like Bees' Knees, Whiz Bang, and Monkey Gland, Pink Lady, Chatterley, Gin and Sin, Golden Slipper and, of course, Green Hat, evoke the world of Michael Arlen. The drinks named after celebrities are dated too: Alfonso XIII, Caruso, Prince of Wales (there is also an Edward VIII), Seapea (C.P. for Cole Porter), Nicky's Fizz (for a Russian prince) and Blue Bird, in honour of Sir Malcolm Campbell.

Frank's Special was a mixture of peach brandy, French vermouth and gin. He notes that he created his Royal to celebrate the opening of the bar, but one suspects a commercial tie-up here, for apart from a dash of angostura bitters, a lump of sugar

[144]

and a slice of lemon peel, the drink consisted of Dry Royal, the brand name of a Loire sparkling wine, and Frank includes the makers' name in his recipe.

George will tell you that people drink less nowadays, so while he will produce a pick-me-up on request there is no call for the wide range of morning-after creations Frank lists. The original Ritz Bar pick-me-up, still in some demand, is composed of orange juice, Cointreau, brandy and champagne. But Frank also offered half a dozen others, including Corpse Revivers No. 1 and 2 (No. 1 was one third each of Applejack or Calvados, brandy and Italian vermouth; No. 2, a glass of Pernod, lemon juice and champagne).

One of Frank's more exotic creations was the Rainbow, which, whatever its appeal to the palate, must have been visually striking. Into a tall liqueur glass one is instructed to pour slowly and carefully, the following ingredients one on top of the other: anisette (pink), mint (green), chartreuse (yellow), cherry brandy (red), kümmel (white), chartreuse (green) and cognac (brown). Care had to be taken to ensure that all the stripes of colour were of equal height in (Frank's description) 'this artistic drink'.

One concoction in Frank's pages he called the Bobby Burns, but I can only think it would have made even that hard-drinking poet revolt at this use of the native whisky he often extolled; it might indeed be called the Scotsman's Nightmare, for it consists of half Scotch whisky, a quarter each French and Italian vermouth and a dash of Benedictine.

But Frank did himself less than justice with the title of *The Artistry of Mixing Drinks*, in that the latter half of his book roams far and wide into a wonderful pot-pourri of information, some of which (such as his chapter on horse-racing and his advice on how to remove finger-marks from furniture) has only a peripheral connection with bar life.

Having sung the praises of the cocktail, Frank unabashedly starts his section on wine (after a prefatory '*Si Dieu nous défendait de boire, aurait-il fait le vin si bon?*') with the statement, 'Wine is justly considered the most wholesome of beverages'. He traces vinous history from Caesar and the early Christians and then goes on to tell his reader what to drink with what and how to serve it, with maps and statistical tables on vineyards and production. Throwing in a few useful definitions (did you know that vermouth comes from the German *Wermut*, or, in English, wormwood?), he passes on to such varied information as, on adjoining pages, what time it is all over the world when it's noon in Paris, and antidotes for poisons. The opening sentence of this second theme is admirable: 'First: send for a physician.'

Frank, as one of his oldest friends and greatest admirers, Rudolf, the head barman of the George V, says fervently at intervals in any conversation on the subject, was a remarkable man.

From old friends like Rudolf one gets an inkling of what made Frank Meier so beloved by a vast circle of people ranging from the cosmopolitan clientele of the Ritz Bar to colleagues in his own trade. He was a stern master but the kindest of friends; at work, genial but dignified and possessed of a phenomenal memory for names and faces.

Rudolf—his surname is Slavik and he is a Bohemian, in the geographical sense—did his military service in the German Army but joined the French Army in 1939. The story he tells which best illustrates Frank's international status is one in which Frank does not himself feature.

Rudolf was a sergeant when he was taken prisoner by the Germans and packed into a train compartment crowded with French officers for the journey to his prison camp. A German officer came in and asked a question to which he replied in German. How did he know German? the officer demanded. Because, said Rudolf, although he lived in Paris he had been born in Prague and had spoken German all his life. He explained that he was a barman.

This interested the German, who then asked him what was the correct way to make an Alexander—cognac or gin? Rudolf told him. Was there a good book on making cocktails? Rudolf suggested that the next time the German was in Paris he should go to the Ritz Bar and ask Frank for a copy. Also, he added, would he give Frank his regards?

The German was impressed and now affable. He gave Rudolf a cigarette. Rudolf broke it and shared it with the man next to him. The German's manner changed. He scowled and said, 'I gave *you* a cigarette—not him.' Rudolf said calmly, 'I am not alone here.' The German glared at him for a moment and then handed out cigarettes all round. Rudolf was the hero of the day. 'All,' he says, 'due to the magic of Frank's name.'

Now, sixteen years after Frank's death, Rudolf is campaigning for a trophy to be awarded by the Bartenders' Guild in Frank's memory. 'Everybody who knew him agrees with me,' he says. 'He was our professor.'

* * *

Many long-time frequenters of the Ritz Bar are unaware that there was ever a time when George Scheuer was *not* in attendance; some will even dispute the point, subconsciously motivated perhaps by an uneasy feeling that the bar and the man could not be separated and survive.

In fact, George's only absence was during the period in the Second World War when, as a French soldier, he was taken prisoner in the north of France in 1940. He escaped and found his way to Marseilles where he worked as a barman, then to Mégève, in Haute Savoie, where he was a *maître d'hôtel*. But, despite the hazards of life for a man of military age in occupied Paris, he was homesick for the Ritz and wrote to M. Auzello asking if his old job would be available if he came back.

When the liberation came he served free champagne to celebrate—and of that great day his most vividly remembered customer was an old friend, Ernest Hemingway, who arrived in his war correspondent's uniform with a Sten gun under his arm ('very wrong,' says George with a smile) and announced that he was 'personally liberating the Ritz'.

This story of the Ritz has become varied and embroidered with legend over the years, but the truth of the matter seems to be that the first arrivals were Colonel (later Ambassador) David Bruce and Hemingway in a jeep. MM. Auzello and Elmiger greeted them. But M. Auzello holds that the real liberation of the Ritz was the previous day when the resident high-ranking Germans left hurriedly ('they had so much loot,' M. Auzello says) and he gave the order to run up the French flag. The first Tricolour broken over Paris was at the Trocadero and M. Auzello claims the Ritz was second. When the news came that many Germans who had taken the wrong route out of Paris in their haste were coming back, M. Auzello was urged to take down the flag but he refused.

Two other distinguished war correspondents, Alan Moorehead and Ted Gilling, arriving like Bruce and Hemingway with the Leclerc division next day, were close on the heels of the American pair. Alan Moorehead says that when they drove up in their Volkswagen, bedecked with pots and pans and bedding rolls, they presented a very un-Ritz-like picture. Neither of them had had a bath for weeks. However, the Ritz received them without so much as a raised eyebrow. 'Will you require rooms?' they were asked politely. In fact they were given suites and celebrated with baths and champagne before they discovered that Hemingway was encamped on the other side of the building, and, of course, joined him.

*　　*　　*

It seemed aptly in the tradition of the Ritz Bar that one day when I arranged to meet George before his work began he arrived late, apologetic but with a perfect excuse. Immaculate in black coat, striped trousers and black pearl-pinned tie, he had been attending the funeral of an old friend, Arturo Lopez, the South American millionaire. 'He was a *grand seigneur*,' said George sadly. 'He was the most polite man I ever knew, always helpful to people in trouble. He was part of my life here. I could have set my watch by his arrival every evening at seven o'clock.'

One of the names always linked with the American expatriate life of the Twenties, and with the Ritz, is F. Scott Fitzgerald. It was he who introduced the newer, younger, less celebrated American writer, Hemingway, to the hotel. Fitzgerald was in the bar every day when he was in Paris and used it many times as a setting in his stories.

There were, of course, times when the erratic Fitzgerald caused George a good deal of trouble. One day he was ordering a drink

when George went over and said, 'Mr Fitzgerald, it cost me a
hundred francs to get that man a new hat.'

'What man?'

'That man whose hat you smashed.'

'Did I smash someone's hat?'

The previous evening Fitzgerald, sitting in the bar, had risen
suddenly and for no apparent reason smashed a stranger's hat.

'I must tell you,' George added, 'that if anything like that
happens again we can't serve you here.'

'You're absolutely right,' said Fitzgerald.

'He always sat in the same place, with his back to the light,'
said George. 'The very place where you are sitting now.' George
shook his head slowly. 'He drank so much,' he said quietly, and
it sounded like the most sympathetic of epitaphs.

If George ever writes his memoirs—which I greatly doubt—
it will be difficult for him to avoid a catalogue of famous names,
a selection of which would include Winston Churchill, the Aga
Khan, an assortment of maharajahs, the legendary dandy,
Mayor Jimmy Walker of New York, Carnegie, Woolworth,
Rockefeller, Pierpont Morgan, Valentino, and Greta Garbo.

Drinking behaviour, as well as drinking tastes, has changed
greatly in George's time. He finds his bar clientele much quieter
than in the between-the-wars years. He hardly ever sees anybody remotely drunk, and is glad of it. He recalls days when
certain customers would come in at noon and stay till ten o'clock
at night.

After the pre-lunch rush hour there used to be a lull, but business would pick up again around five, by six the bar would be
distinctly busy and by seven o'clock it would be full. Five o'clock
used to be the time when people thought about cocktails; now
the bar is liable to be empty at five and it is at least an hour and a
half later before the real influx begins and the bar may not be
really busy till nearly eight. Then most of the customers will
have a few drinks and go off to dinner. 'The old American two-
fisted drinker has disappeared,' the American columnist, John
Crosby, recently reported nostalgically after talking to George.
'At least he's disappeared from the Ritz, which was his hangout.

The American, in short, is getting Europeanised in his drinking habits.'

George has a reputation for being able to get or fix anything. For example, an American in Paris just after the war told a friend of mine that he had always wanted to have a copper bathtub and had never been able to find one in America, although they were once highly esteemed. He figured that they had been introduced to the U.S. by or at the time of Lafayette, and he had hoped he could get one in France. He had tried all the normal sources and antique dealers without success. My friend gave him a note of introduction to George and in ten days he had a copper bathtub, which he shipped back to the U.S.

Sometimes the customer's desires can be freakishly whimsical. A man once remarked in the bar that he had always wanted an elephant tusk. George quickly produced one for him.

There is a story of Cole Porter wanting to transport a piano to a friend's apartment in the early hours of the morning. George found a truck and willing driver. Of course, people come to lean on a man like George, but he seems to enjoy it. There have been cases where a diplomat, suddenly posted, has simply said, 'George, sell my car for me, will you?' and handed him the keys. Next time in Paris, he is greeted by George—and the proceeds of the sale.

One old friend and admirer of George said to me solemnly, 'If you should ever be unfortunate enough to go to jail in Paris it is as well to let George know. He likes to send something—a dish of *bisque de homard* perhaps—to his friends in trouble.

* * *

The third bar of the Ritz was opened only last year. To differentiate between *the* bar—George's headquarters—and Bertin's bar across the lobby, the newcomer is 'the Vendôme cocktail lounge' or 'the garden bar'. Its creation was M. Auzello's idea, springing from the feeling that while the other bars are adjacent to the grill-room on the Cambon side the hotel restaurant should have a bar close by, so that people who want to dine in the restaurant need not cross the long gallery to the other side of the hotel.

The new bar usurps no space which was usefully employed before; it simply occupies the Vendôme end of the garden which flanks the restaurant and in daylight its whole exterior wall of window presents the long vista of the garden.

It is deliberately quite different in style from the other bars. It is panelled in light Oregon pine and its chairs are in what appears, to eye or touch, to be tan and yellow leather but is, in fact, a plastic on jersey, which makes it non-wrinkling. There are English hunting prints on the walls. The usual Ritz meticulousness about detail went into the making of the new bar—mathematical calculations of how high (or low) the tables and chairs should be in relation to the height of the roof; endless experimentation with shades of green for the carpet so that it would suggest the garden theme without being obtrusively strong; the decision to have no bottles on show but the drink in fine decanters on glass shelves, backed with mirror, at the back of the bar.

But a more revolutionary, and even more elaborate, recent operation was the redesigning and redecoration of the main bar early this year. Many old customers were appalled at the idea that *the* Ritz Bar should be altered one iota from the way it had been for twenty-seven years, but in M. Ritz's words, 'The lighting and general atmosphere no longer corresponded to what we thought the clientele requires and would like.'

There was nothing half-hearted about the change; as usual with the Ritz, the planning was scrupulously detailed. The transformation was predicated on two essential requirements: 'cosiness', which it was felt the old bar lacked, and a form of lighting which, as M. Ritz crisply puts it, 'glamorises women'.

The problem with the first requirement was to achieve 'cosiness' without loss of space, particularly cubic space, which means air. The room is exceptionally high-ceilinged, so an *apparent* reduction of height was the first aim. A false balcony was introduced round the sides and a wire-mesh dome installed in the middle. As the night-sky effect in L'Espadon had been successful, it was decided to employ a variation of this in the bar. The upper walls and balcony were painted with a fluorescent paint and two lighting systems devised—one for day and one

[151]

for night. Thus a sunny effect was obtained in daylight and at night black light tubes produced a luminous effect on the ceiling and upper walls—'a tropical light,' M. Ritz says, giving 'the idea of escape and relaxation which a tropical atmosphere induces'.

The resolution of the lighting problem enthused M. Ritz to new heights of technical expertise (in which he delights) and he is duly proud of the fact that the new installation is the first of its kind in France—a patent 'electronic light-stabilising regulator' which enables the illumination to be graded at will from zero to maximum candle-power and which he claims as 'the greatest technical innovation in lighting in years'.

A feature of the old bar was the mural painting, and for a while M. Ritz puzzled over what should replace this. Eventually when he and the decorator, M. Carlhian, were in Venice they saw in one of the old palaces a mirror of smoky glass with an *appliqué* design in crystal. This was the inspiration for a glass-covered wall which now faces the entrance to the bar, adding depth and perspective. M. Carlhian produced a design representing the Chateau de Chantilly and this was executed by the famous glass-makers of the island of Murano. These craftsmen also made the opaque crystal-glass which filters the light from shallow columns on the walls of the bar.

The same painstaking care went into the choice of every detail—the silvered bronze table-legs, the green silk brocade for the chairs (with others in black horsehair for contrast), the hand-lacquered table-tops in different colours, even the matching Venetian glassware to hold potato crisps. For all the Ritz's conservatism, the 'total scheme' of the bar is admitted to be 'somewhat advanced technically', but this was a deliberate policy, based on the belief that it could be carried out with taste and style and also on the realisation that the merely 'new' is apt to become quickly outmoded.

No ambiance could have been created with more loving care, but the great Frank's creed has been remembered too: that the essence of a bar is not decoration or drink—he called that simply 'the bond of good fellowship'—but people. For forty years the words 'Ritz Bar' have meant people.

CHAPTER NINE

THE WHEELS GO ROUND

AN HOTEL is a business, and a famous luxury hotel, however much it strives to preserve the personal touch and the dignity of a stately home, is big business. The provision of shelter, sustenance and service remains the simple root of the matter, but time and success inevitably create around that root a commercial complex of considerable magnitude. As a property and a 'going concern' business what does the Ritz amount to?

The hotel consists, physically and financially, of a plot of land a little over an acre in area (4,170 square metres, of which two-fifths are gardens) which, together with the buildings standing on it, has a value on paper of about half a million pounds.

The hotel contains about £100,000 worth of furnishings and the 'grand valuation' of assets, as shown in the company's accounts filed with the registrar of companies in London, is £832,350, or roughly seven times the original capital with which César Ritz launched his venture. But it must be stressed that these valuations are 'on paper' and an expert estimate of the true value today, keeping in mind that all the land does not belong to the company, puts it conservatively at £2,500,000. The goodwill of the Ritz is anybody's guess.

The fact that the Ritz does not own all its property brings up one of the most surprising things about the hotel's situation: strictly speaking, though it is not likely to happen, the Ritz could lose about half its premises at short notice. This comes about because of events centring on the hotel's acquisition of the extra property in the Place Vendôme and the Rue Cambon which enabled it to expand from the original eighty-odd rooms of César's hotel to its present 210.

In 1912 the house next door to the hotel, No. 17 Place Vendôme, and a property to the rear, fronting on the Rue Cambon and then consisting of stables and coach houses, came into the market. The Ritz hoped to buy these properties but learned that a neighbour in the Rue Cambon, the powerful French bank, Crédit Foncier, was also interested. The Ritz directors decided it would be foolish and futile to bid against the bank, so an arrangement was reached by which, when the bank had bought the properties, it would lease them to the Ritz and would also provide a loan for building. The lease was for forty years and repayment of the loan was due on expiry of the lease.

Soon after the end of the First World War, the Crédit Foncier intimated that in view of the devaluation of the franc it would require repayment of the loan in gold. The Ritz replied that this was impossible and the matter was taken to court. Judgment was given in favour of the Ritz, but the court held that the presence of the payment-in-gold clause in the lease made it invalid. Thus the Ritz was in the position of having built an hotel on land to which it had no rights. The bank then delivered its ultimatum: knock down the hotel or accept the lease offered. The Ritz had no choice. They had been paying a rent of 275,000 francs a year, of which 200,000 was recovered from the shops belonging to the property in the Place Vendôme. The Crédit Foncier now demanded the formidable rent of two million francs a year. The Ritz finally reached a settlement by which they turned the profitable shops back to the Crédit Foncier and a net annual rent of 990,000 francs was fixed. The new lease replaced the original, or invalid, one, and this expired in 1952. There was a first extension to 1962 and a second which runs to the end of 1971.

The hotel's situation is not quite so precarious as the bare facts sound, for French law would provide for substantial compensation if a going concern were threatened with extinction through such a cause as the withholding of a renewal of lease and, to do justice to the bank, it has never been suggested that they have had the faintest desire or intention to dispossess their distinguished tenants.

The original capital of the Ritz was £120,500 in 24,000 ordinary shares of £5 each and 100 deferred shares of £5 each. In 1906 it was increased to £175,000 divided into 35,000 shares of £5 each.

In 1933 the board obtained powers to repay £2 of the capital paid-up on each of the issued shares. Stockholders thus received £2 tax-free on each £5 share and the remaining £3 was divided into three £1 shares. Thus an original holder of 100 shares worth £500 received £200 cash and now held 300 £1 shares of ever-increasing value. In 1957 the capital was increased by issuing one bonus 'C' (non-voting) share for every £1 share held. Ritz shares very rarely change hands.

The board of directors of the Ritz is now composed of Charles Ritz (chairman), M. Auzello (managing director), Lady Berlin (née Aline de Gunzbourg, wife of Sir Isaiah Berlin, the Oxford don), Sir George Bracewell Smith (who among other things is chairman of the London Ritz-Carlton group of hotels and a former Lord Mayor of London), M. Edouard Vernes, a banker, M. Auguste Lambiotte, a Belgian industrialist with big interests in France, and Mr W. H. Taylor, the former secretary-general of the company.

Hardly a month goes by without the board receiving an offer to buy the business. Usually they pay no attention, but when occasionally they take the trouble to find out who has ambitions to take them over they discover that the offer comes from a middleman or nominee representing some well-known individual or group in the world of international finance, almost always American.

*　　*　　*

If César Ritz had not fallen ill in his prime—if he had, for instance, continued in active business for another twenty years, thereby attaining no more than the present age of his notably energetic son—he would undoubtedly have become the first of a new breed of hoteliers, the international hotel tycoon. He had no intention of merely cultivating his first Ritz Hotel when he had achieved it, though it would certainly always have occupied a special place in his affections, and its first successor, the London Ritz, was indeed a reality before his enforced retirement. His plans spanned the civilised world and as his achievements rarely fell short of his ambitions there would surely have been by the 1920s a chain of Ritz hotels from Istanbul to Tokyo, Athens to Los Angeles. (There *are* many other Ritz hotels, such as those in London, Montreal, Madrid, Barcelona and Lisbon, for example, but none of them is owned by the Paris Ritz although Charles Ritz is on the board of the London and Lisbon hotels.)

It would have been interesting to see how César would have coped with drastically changing conditions and if his heirs had succeeded to such a chain as he might have created their task would have continued to present them with formidable problems, for the hotel chains which do exist nowadays operate on principles and policies very different from those of Ritz. In this, of course, hotels are basically no different from other forms of commerce; they are simply more personal.

All costs have increased vastly—city and state taxes, and labour costs most of all. (Hotel charges, incidentally, have not increased proportionately.) This factor alone would have revolutionised the approach to de luxe hotel economics. Ritz's policy was to supply the service he regarded as essential without counting the cost; now the chain-hotel policy is to supply a standard service based, with actuarial precision, on cost.

When a modern hotel-chain operator approaches a new project he goes in with his figures already fixed; that is, so much capital outlay, so much revenue per room, and therefore so much allocated for cost of staff. This slide-rule approach dictates the number of staff to be employed strictly economically and not primarily in terms of service. Thus the calculation of permitted expenditure against potential revenue may allow—as in a recent actual case—a staff of 700 for an hotel of more than 500 rooms with a capacity of over 800 guests.

The Ritz still approaches this question from the other end: what staff is essential for what is considered proper service? The

Ritz staff at full strength numbers 460, or approximately 2½ per guest when the hotel is full; at quiet times, like early February, for instance, even the seasonally reduced staff is often in the ratio of four servants to every guest. The contrast is not to be over-simplified as simply extravagance versus economy, the old-fashioned lavish against the streamlined modern. It is rather more psychological than commercial. A Ritz is staffed for the rush hours of the day; many hotels are staffed for the non-rush hours. This is why, on arrival at a chain-hotel at the same time as others, a guest may wait an hour for his luggage to be delivered to his room. Nobody is being dilatory or forgetful; the hotel has almost certainly a carefully worked-out system, but this is as quickly as the available staff can deal with the job. Obviously some guests will be lucky and have prompt, or reasonably prompt, delivery of their luggage, but others will have to wait their turn.

What is liable to suffer most by modern chain-hotel methods is floor service. This has always tended to be uneconomic, but in the Ritz tradition it is the essential test of an hotel. The Ritz faces the fact that it is not uncommon for the number of meals served in rooms in the course of twenty-four hours to be less than the number of floor waiters employed.

The staff wages bill is the biggest difference between the running of an hotel now and a generation ago, and the difference does not by any means all go into the pay-packets of the employees. In France today every 100 francs paid to an employee costs the hotel approximately 140 francs. 'Social charges', as they are called, account for the extra forty per cent. These include health and accident insurance and a tax per head of personnel. The Ritz wages bill in 1962 was £200,000, the largest single item of the hotel's expenditure (42·5 per cent of the total), but in addition to the 40 per cent 'social charges' it has to be remembered that the staff also receive the 15 per cent service charge added to every bill and not included in the £200,000 mentioned above.

I asked Bernard Penché, the *secrétaire-général*, if he did not sometimes envy his predecessors in his job, if he did not find modern hotel accounting very complicated.

'Yes,' he said, 'I sometimes wish we had the old wages sheets.

They were much simpler. In 1914 there was just a figure and a signature. Now there are seventeen columns. There should be more, but the accounting machines won't take any more.'

*　　*　　*

Even in these complicated days the trading account of the Ritz is, in general terms, almost as simple as that of any inn. Letting rooms provides 48 per cent of the hotel's income and the restaurants and bars 46 per cent. The remaining 6 per cent comes from investments.

On the expenditure side everything except the purchases of food and wine (17 per cent of the total) is a series of constant outgoings which continue, day in, day out, irrespective of the business transacted, and these run up a daily bill of £1,100. On a turnover of £806,000 in 1962 the breakdown of 'where the money went' is as follows:

Salaries, wages, etc.	42·5 per cent
Taxes	11
Running expenses, maintenance and renewals	26
Purchase of food and drink	17
Profit	3·5
	100

It was César Ritz who determined to liberate his hotel managers from their ledgers and his son Charles who rebelled against hotel guests being blinded with graph paper. César ruled that a manager, to do his job properly, must delegate the detailed book-keeping, though of course surpervising the results, and it was his son, in one of his early training jobs far away from the Ritz, who instituted the hotel bill which shows only seven days on the page.

Mechanisation came after César's time, but this is one department in which the Ritz has deliberately broken with tradition, though care is taken to see that the guest is never aware of it. Bills are still hand-written, the machine-printed bill being regarded as too impersonal; but the information on it is produced by backroom comptometer and computer, the clatter of which never penetrates beyond the office door. Even Penché, the head backroom boy of the Ritz, admits only a hint of automation to show in his own office over the staff entrance in the Rue Cambon. There is on his desk a discreetly small calculating machine. But distilled into the analyses of the hotel's housekeeping, which are always within Penché's reach, are the products of the unseen machines.

Penché is thirty-six and has been in his present position for seven years. He was born in Le Mans and on leaving school started out to be a teacher but was attracted by the hotel business and at seventeen went to a specialised hotel training school for two years. He trained in the kitchens and as a waiter and he also learned hotel accounting. In 1946 he joined the Ritz by simply writing and asking for an interview. He recalls that when he was waiting, by the time-clock at the staff entrance, the doorman said, ' If you get a job you'll either be here for under six months or a lifetime.' Now, seventeen years later, it looks like being a lifetime, for long service is common in the Ritz. A few years ago, when it was decided to give medals to members of the staff with twenty-five years' service or more, the number qualifying was 101.

The job Penché got at the Ritz was bill office clerk and his rise might be dated from the time when Mr Taylor, the then secretary-general, picked him to go to London for further training and to perfect his English. He worked in reception at Brown's Hotel and spent nine months in the office of the Ritz's accountants—the same firm who sent Mr Taylor to the Ritz in 1916, a sojourn from which he never returned. It was as Mr Taylor's assistant that Penché returned to the Ritz and six years later he was held to be the natural choice as the secretary-general's successor.

It is very much in the tradition of César Ritz to keep a watchful eye on the younger generation of staff to ensure that the right men are in training for the top jobs when the need arises to fill them. Just as César tapped Henri Elles and Victor Rey when they were in relatively minor positions and had them ready for the managership in due course, so today there is Penché, well on the right side of forty and already an experienced secretary-general, and Zembrzuski, just over fifty (a later starter because of the war), both of whom were selected when clerks and are now at least the most likely heirs-apparent for the executive direction of a business whose present top men are in their seventies.

M. Auzello attaches great importance to the office of secretary-general. He variously compares the job with that of Chief of Staff in military terms or Auditor-General in government. It is very far removed, he emphasises, from a simple matter of accountancy. Switching to a theatrical metaphor, he said to me one day, 'One must always give due importance to the people behind the scenes, whether it is the secretary, the chef or the cellarman. Others are "on stage" but they are back-stage and get no applause. The secretary-general is one of the most important people in the show. The management cannot see everything and it is the secretary-general's job to draw attention to what is going on in the back-stage administration. I always listened very carefully to Mr Taylor in the long years when he was my close collaborator and friend. I was always anxious to be sure that what I was doing was all right from his point of view. I passed on many problems to him and so ensured that the two sides of the business were always in complete co-operation—as I do now with Penché. And although Mr Taylor is semi-retired, he always has my ear and I still listen very carefully to him.'

It is almost literally true to say that Penché has the vital statistics of the Ritz at his finger-tips, for he has only to slip his hand into his breast pocket to produce the precise answer to almost any question. He carries at all times his *carnet*—a small, loose-leaf diary in the back pages of which he has, for immediate reference, the vital statistics of his stewardship. He can tell you, with the speed of a quiz kid, how many people are staying in the hotel, how many dinners were served last night in the restaurant, the grill-room, and on the floors, and what the food bills for the day and the current month are, set against the comparative figures for the same day and month of the previous year.

The *carnet* is really an abstract of the daily reports which Penché studies every morning. Not only do the comparisons with the equivalent period last year show how the turnover, and therefore the profit, are running, but also errors of accountancy can be detected and significant trends brought to light and reported to M. Auzello.

A major discrepancy is revealed at a glance; the Ritz's turnover is generally very steady and therefore if this year's figure for a particular item is substantially different from last year it is worth investigating. For example, on a day when I examined the report the purchase price of meat was 19,865 francs and the comparative figure for the previous year was 19,735 francs.

Each category of expenditure is listed as a percentage of the total. In the case of the meat item the current figure was 10·1 per cent as against 10·09 per cent the previous year. If the variation had been much greater, with the number of meals served roughly the same, the explanation might have been that meat was dearer in the market. But if this were not so then there was either over-buying or waste, or the book-keeping had slipped up.

This remarkable consistency of consumption was illustrated by another basic purchase—bread. Again the variation from one year to the next was no more than a hundredth of one per cent—3·34 per cent (96,202 francs) against 3·33 per cent (or 97,403 francs).

Not only are day-to-day purchases of food and numbers of guests in the house remarkably steady from one year to the next but, except when some major alterations or redecorations are being done, so are the maintenance costs. The bills for maintenance and replacements of carpets, curtains and upholstery run at a fairly consistent £10,000 a year (the Ritz's old linen goes to the makers of high-quality playing cards) and breakages at £2,000 a year. The formidable costs involved nowadays are well illustrated by the fact that when the curtains in a small reading-room were recently taken down for cleaning it was suggested that they might be renewed, but it was found that the cost of replacement would be £750. Even the simple glass ashtrays which (other hotels might profitably copy) are profusely supplied in every room, public or private, require replacement at the rate of 2,000 a year.

This is not entirely through breakage; even Ritz guests sometimes like souvenirs. (Even more surprising at the Ritz is that
pepper-mills also disappear with distressing frequency. 'And
they are much dearer than ashtrays,' Auzello says.)

Any sensible hotelier is always watching out for possible
economies which will not reduce the service or standards of the
hotel, but even when Penché spots such a chance he often holds
his hand for what can only be called Ritz reasons. One case of
this was the hand-made light switches; they, like the cut-velvet
fabric which covers the restaurant chairs, are maintained as
in César's time, despite the difficulty of procuring them and the
vastly increased cost. Each time a dining-room chair is recovered it costs £20. Penché's analysis of the maintenance of
these chairs shows that it works out at a shilling per meal served.

*   *   *

If Penché is the backroom boy responsible for making the unseen wheels of the Ritz go round smoothly, his frontroom
opposite number is the resident manager, Janusz Zembrzuski,
a tall, slim fifty-year-old Polish ex-diplomat. Instead of the
figures and analyses which occupy the secretary-general behind
the scenes, people—whether clientele or staff—are the resident
manager's first concern, and although he does much of his work
back-stage he is always at the disposal of the guests. Indeed
Zembrzuski, under the jurisdiction of the managing director, is
the man primarily responsible for personifying the Ritz tradition
of 'the personal touch'.

But in a modern hotel this is less easy than it once was and
Zembrzuski has to be much more than a greeter and soother.
He firmly places 'the comfort and happiness of the guests' as his
essential task, but with the increased transience of guests—three
weeks is quite a long stay now whereas three months was once
common—he finds he cannot make contact with everybody, and
although he joined the Ritz as relatively recently as 1946 he is
so imbued with the spirit of the place that he worries over this.

The two sides, the seen and the unseen, of the manager's work
often clash or overlap. He cannot tell guests that he has more

important things to do than discuss which theatre or art show they should go to; he must make them feel his time is theirs although he knows there is a pile of essential work waiting in his office.

'Always,' he told me, 'I try to remember that the guests' requirements, however trivial, must be met, even their whims fulfilled if possible, for it is on that side of the job that I and the hotel will be judged.'

Zembrzuski's years with the Polish diplomatic service were an ideal, if accidental, training for the hotel business. Like most careers, his has had its element of chance. He was private secretary to the Polish Under-Secretary of State for Foreign Affairs for five years before the war, then went into the army, and eventually to Switzerland. The Ritz's then chairman, Colonel Pfyffer, had a Polish wife and at her home in Switzerland she frequently entertained the displaced Poles.

In 1946, Zembrzuski, having decided not to go back to Poland, was in Paris and looking for a job. He had come no nearer to deciding on a career than wondering in what line a diplomatic training would be of most use.

One day he had a message from Hans Elmiger, who had heard of him from his aunt, Colonel Pfyffer's wife. Would he like a job as a summer holiday replacement at the reception desk of the Ritz? He took it, enjoyed it, was asked to stay on and seven months later was appointed head receptionist. When the post of resident manager became vacant both Elmiger and Auzello, the managing director, decided without hesitation that Zembrzuski, in spite of his brief experience, was the man for the job. Zembrzuski now lives in a flat at the top of the hotel with his English wife and deploys all his diplomatic charm and skill in an exhausting but fascinating job.

He brought to his job absolutely no knowledge of hotel-keeping, but he had a knowledge of the world which was lacking in more experienced receptionists. He was brought up, he says, in 'a certain atmosphere' which gave him a natural politeness and an ability to see a business in terms of human beings whose point of view he instinctively sought to understand.

[163]

At the Ritz he saw that the 'human' approach, which was natural to him, was in the Ritz tradition. 'In a different type of hotel,' he says, 'I might easily have been a failure.' So far as is possible he tries to receive and handle the customers as though they were his guests in a private house. This is only possible to a limited extent, as no host could be expected to have to deal with guests as difficult, demanding, exacting and even sometimes downright unreasonable as hotel guests can be.

When the number of guests was smaller, because they stayed longer, the customers of the *luxe* hotel were spoiled, their every whim catered for, their tastes (as well as their eccentricities) remembered and anticipated on each visit. Nowadays, with greater numbers and shorter stays, the cosseting cannot be so thorough, though there are still, of course, exceptions. But, in general, every guest expects to be satisfied to the last detail and it is the manager's task to see that this expectation is fulfilled.

Zembrzuski has no rules, apart from politeness and as thoughtful a personal service as possible. He works on instinct and intuition. Sometimes he thinks he gets undue credit for handling people or situations when all he has done is behave naturally as an *homme du monde*. He does not want to be thought of as a miracle-worker. He doesn't want to have to do 'anything spectacular'; only make the wheels go round smoothly, and, as he says, 'to avoid incidents which might turn into catastrophe'. He aims to please and gratify, within reasonable bounds. He knows that guests expect much of the Ritz. Too much? He smiles, shrugs and says, 'There is no perfection in this world, but there are ways of saying "no" that are not unpleasant.'

Here again the maxim of the customer always being right is subject to modification. One day recently Zembrzuski was going out of the hotel when a receptionist called to him. Zembrzuski recognised it as a desperate cry for help. A man had arrived on his first visit to the hotel and announced that the sitting-room of his suite was too small and not at all what he expected at the Ritz. He had been complaining loud and long and the receptionist had been quite unable to pacify him.

Zembrzuski looked at the correspondence about the booking

and then tackled the angry guest. This was not a case for soft words. Zembrzuski countered with a simple statement, but he put it quite sharply. 'Look,' he said in effect. 'Your booking was made by a travel agent. He simply asked for a suite. He did not specify a large sitting-room. We had no knowledge of you or your tastes. Would you have liked it if we had imposed a very expensive suite on you?'

He then took the guest and showed him one of the three so-called royal suites; the sitting-rooms are large—almost formidably so—and so are the prices. The difference in price was about £10 a day. The man agreed that he would not have wanted anything so vast, grand and costly. The tone of the conversation changed. The guest accepted the realities of the situation and Zembrzuski sent flowers to his wife.

While obeying his intuitions, Zembrzuski says he employs a different tone to different cases.

*   *   *

Zembrzuski's daily routine begins when he comes down from his apartment at 8.30 a.m. He goes to M. Auzello's office, where the morning's mail is waiting, and they discuss the action to be taken on it. He next moves round to reception and deals with the mail received there, mainly bookings and questions of room availability and allocation. He then retires to his office and dictates anything up to sixty letters. Next he turns to staff problems, which are unending. But by this time guests' personal matters are beginning to come up and he may spend the rest of the morning dealing with these in person or on the telephone. A particularly time-consuming service is advising guests on which hotels they should stay in other countries, and he will even do their booking for them.

He lunches in his flat between one o'clock and two, coming down in time for a tour of inspection of the restaurant and grill-room to see that all is going well with the luncheon guests. Clear of that, and having taken on perhaps a half-a-dozen personal chores for guests who have buttonholed him over their lunches, he goes on to inspecting and checking work in progress, for there

is always something being built or renovated in the hotel. Back
in his office he deals with the afternoon mail, signs his letters,
checks those he has dictated for M. Auzello's signature and on a
rare and lucky day he retires upstairs at his official finishing time
of seven p.m., but of course still on call if required.

* * *

The 'individual approach' of the Ritz to its guests extends to a
system of advance booking which is unusual if not unique.
Normally, when you write or telegraph to an hotel, for, say, a
double room for next June, you will receive a reply that there is
or is not a vacancy. This is done on a purely numerical basis;
that is, if there are forty unbooked rooms forty more reservations
will be accepted and the forty-first will be unlucky. The forty
bookings will be 'juggled' as to specific allocations nearer the
time.

But the Ritz keeps forward-booking registers which, in fact,
record bookings not yet made. The effect of this, in practice, is
that if you liked a particular room over one of the gardens when
you were last in Paris and you write to the Ritz seeking to book it
again for a visit the following summer, Zembrzuski may find, on
referring to the register, 'Mr and Mrs Smith' pencilled in with a
wiggly line drawn down through the two weeks of June that you
want. This means that, while no reservation has been made,
Mr and Mrs Smith usually, or at least frequently, come for those
two June weeks and they are given an unasked-for priority. You
will be offered another room, but if Mr Smith has not been heard
from by about February, the Ritz will write and ask if he is
proposing to come this year. If he says no, then *you* will be asked
if you would still like the accommodation you had in mind as it is
now available.

All this requires a lot of correspondence and much care and
thought, but it is a personal service and the Ritz finds it worth
while. It means that quick bookings are not always possible; the
Ritz does not like sudden telephone calls demanding a firm,
immediate answer. These advance registers, Zembrzuski said to
me, 'are the conscience of the Ritz, our conscience towards

people whom we know and have been good customers in the past. We cannot always answer quickly because we have to consult these books—and reflect. Reservations require reflection.'

* * *

A man who runs an hotel tackles problems in applied psychology daily, and many recur so regularly that he deals with them automatically. But one problem which remains irksome and embarrassing will probably go on cropping up at intervals so long as human nature does not change. This is the morals (or possible lack of morals) of his clientele. In a country like France, where the law requires an hotel to register full identity particulars of everybody sleeping under its roof, it becomes a question of making rules and sticking to them; it is not possible (as it is in England, where the native need produce no papers whatever) to deny all knowledge of whether a man and a woman sharing a room are married or not.

The Ritz rules are simple and strictly applied, but naturally people react differently to them. Two people of opposite sex whose papers do not show them to be married may not occupy one room, or even two rooms *en suite* where one is a sitting-room. If a man who has booked one bedroom, with or without sitting-room, turns up with a woman who is not his wife, the receptionist reports to the manager who confronts the man privately and puts it to him bluntly: the lady must have another room elsewhere in the hotel. Curiously enough, this rarely gives rise to any trouble. The manager may take the edge off the ultimatum by saying, 'You may think us old-fashioned or ridiculous, but we have our rules.' Anyhow this is one case where the manager does not mind having a row if necessary.

One quite common reaction is for the man to object to producing passports or papers on the grounds that it's an absurd formality and doesn't matter. In this event the manager produces the magic word 'police'—from whom the registration rules emanate —and that is the end of the matter.

But the man-with-the-woman-not-his-wife still represents the situation the hotel manager most dislikes and in which he tries to use his highest degree of delicate diplomacy to sort it out without fuss. Of course, there are hotels which don't strive so hard; the Ritz attitude to them is 'Look at the clientele they get—*and* the reputation.'

The Ritz is prepared to admit that it doesn't like film stars, and their entourages, as resident guests, but, of course, it is also prepared to make exceptions. For example, Charlie Chaplin is regarded as a sort of world-citizen man of distinction, and therefore an honoured guest. Audrey Hepburn is a 'lady' first and a film star only incidentally; her *chic*, her good manners; are more important than her celebrity as an actress. The hotel's attitude to Miss Hepburn, only this side of infatuation, is illustrated by the fact that her film with Gary Cooper, *Love in the Afternoon*, was filmed with the full co-operation of the Ritz and partly shot in the hotel, although no such facilities had ever been given before.

There is a firm distinction, incidentally, between film stars and film magnates. Some of the great names of Hollywood—Zukor, Goldwyn, Loew, Warner—have been and are regular visitors, and Sir Alexander Korda was an habitué. The difference is that the magnates do not attract what M. Auzello described to me as 'exuberant publicity', which is what the Ritz shrinks from.

But, as the generalisation was put succinctly to me, film stars 'don't fit' at the Ritz and are not encouraged. One managerial executive confided that his own reactions had even surprised himself: one day he saw a famous international star coming into the hotel and instinctively he thought how glad he was that when in Paris she chooses to stay elsewhere. ('She was wearing a red dress,' he said, 'but it was *so* red. It looked quite wrong in the Ritz.') He freely admits that he thinks this particular star very beautiful and has often admired her on the screen. In other words he is prepared to acknowledge all her qualities—so long as they are displayed outside his hotel.

There *have* been times when film personalities have stayed at the Ritz and all has gone well, but there have been occasions which seem to justify the management's resistance to this clientele. One man with a famous name wired from Rome a few hours after leaving and asked for his clothes to be sent on. There was some mystification about why he hadn't taken his clothes until it was found that they were all floating in a full bathtub in his suite. As he was known to be a drinker, it was decided that he must have fallen into some confusion about packing late the previous night. The hotel politely wired that his clothes would be sent on as soon as they had been dried and pressed. He was not able to make a reservation at the Ritz again.

Inevitably, illness and death occur in hotels, but their presence must not be intruded upon the other guests. When a very difficult old lady was mortally ill Zembrzuski called on her twice a day, interrupting more important work, because if he beguiled her with social conversation and soothed over her complaints— which were constant and largely imaginary—they did not fall on the rest of the staff and so make more trouble all round.

I had been told that on the unfortunate occasions when death occurs on the premises Zembrzuski has a system of getting the corpses out of the hotel so unobtrusively as to amount to a sort of macabre sleight-of-hand. One senior member of the staff told me that in all his time at the hotel he had never seen a glimpse of one of those removals, nor had he ever been able to discover how it was done.

Zembrzuski was amused when I told him this. He smiled and shrugged and simply said, 'It is the sort of thing I would never have thought of as remarkable. It is just routine. One does not bring a coffin in or take it out by the front door in the middle of the day. One does it quietly, discreetly—that is all.'

The same discretion surrounds the business of security. The Ritz has a chief house detective (an ex-policeman who does not look like one) who has a small day-and-night staff. In a sense they are spies—and just as anxious as spies not to be spotted for what they are. But you might find out what one looked like if you were to wander around the hotel at the wrong times and in the wrong places—or perhaps evince a persistent inclination to get into conversation with strangers in the bar. I gather that what would seem like just another guest would discreetly approach and inquire if he could help you in—well, whatever might be your business.

[169]

Zembrzuski is frank about the fact that occasionally, though not often, even at the Ritz, an hotel manager has to swallow insults. Usually, he says, you keep your temper by thinking how un-dignified is the behaviour of the insulter—and in the knowledge that you will have the upper hand later. Some incidents fall into a repeating pattern. There is the lost watch, or piece of jewellery, which is reported just as guests are about to leave. Zembrzuski offers to supervise an expert search of rooms and luggage. When this is agreed, the missing article almost invariably turns up. But sometimes the guest refuses—and is rude about it. He *knows* the missing article isn't in the room or in his bags, and, what is more, he is satisfied that it has been stolen by the staff. If people like Zembrzuski were more careful to employ honest staff. . . .

In such cases one of two things usually happens. A thorough search after the guest has gone brings the lost article to light, or (and this happens with almost boring consistency) a telegram or letter arrives with profuse apologies; the missing article *was* in the luggage after all. The Ritz keeps a special file devoted to such documents.

* * *

Zembrzuski is not one of those hirers of labour who criticise the staff for not being prepared to be the slaves they once were. 'Hotel life *is* a kind of slavery,' he says. 'It's no use trying to force people into the discipline of it unless they have a feeling for service. They can make more money in industry and have better hours—a five-day week and more home life. My heart sinks when a good, experienced floor waiter, for instance, comes and tells me he is leaving, but I can't blame him.'

Floor service at the Ritz could not go on but for the young German, Italian and Spanish waiters who, when they finish training in their own country, go to Paris for experience and to improve their French. There is, of course, a cachet in having worked at the Ritz—Charles Ritz, with a hint of irritation, calls it the 'Ritz certificate'—which some of the short-staying staff like to acquire.

But the foreign labour available and eager to work at the Ritz is no complete solution. There would be a higher proportion of foreign waiters but for the fact that the law lays down strict conditions for their employment. They must be trainees, under thirty, with three years' experience in their own country, and they are granted a work permit for six months which is renewable only twice, making a maximum of eighteen months' employment. Thus the management has the galling task of letting good waiters go and finding new ones in a constant turnover. Zembrzuski lives in a state of permanent prayer that the flow will not dry up.

The French waiter is, of course, still the basis of the Ritz service. The Frenchman has a strong streak of independence in his nature and does not obey orders dumbly, as his opposite numbers of some races do. He has to be convinced that what he is being told to do is practical, sensible and necessary; then, in the opinion of the Ritz management, he usually does it better than anybody else. But he has to be handled with finesse.

The most transient of all staff the hotel hires are the dish-washers. This is the one sector where the manager will not claim to know his personnel by name or even by sight. He is resigned to the fact that dish-washers come and go in an ever-changing procession; they may stay for a day or a few weeks and then vanish. Rarely does one give formal notice. Again Zembrzuski is sympathetic rather than critical.

Otherwise the biggest turnover in staff is in pageboys, but for different reasons. They tend to grow out of the job, not only literally but in other ways. Whereas they used to stay on and graduate to other jobs, often as *chasseurs*, they now make enough money to enable them to move on to other, more profitable fields.

Usually they come from working-class families and are recommended by members of the staff. Arriving as fourteen-year-old urchins to whom the world of the Ritz must be bewildering, they are apt to become rapidly very smart, sometimes excessively so. One boy who had been at the hotel only a few weeks was found to be selling used razor-blade containers, gleaned from waste-paper baskets, to a new boy, telling him that these were very important and guests would pay well for them. This bright boy developed altogether too fast: he was betting on horses, chasing girls and, out of uniform, was becoming alarmingly dressy on the lines that Paris shop advertisements sometimes describe as '*chic, presque snob*'. He had to go, but nobody was in the least worried about his future.

Sometimes swift physical growth and quickly acquired worldliness combine to produce surprising results. One particularly diminutive boy was obviously very poor when he came. When he was told to go on an errand on a bicycle it was found he was too small to reach the pedals. A few months later he was arriving at work on his own motor-scooter.

All the bright boys are eager to learn languages; a smattering of the customer's tongue tends to produce good tips. There was one boy who liked to try out newly acquired English words on me, checking for meaning or pronunciation. One day he took me up in the lift and when we reached the landing he looked around conspiratorially to make sure we were alone then said, 'Please, sir, *écoutez*'—and quietly sang right through 'It's a Long, Long Way to Tipperary' with a baby-Chevalier accent.

When there is a complaint against a servant an unvarying procedure is employed. The accused is sent for. 'You know Monsieur X in Room Z?' says the manager. 'I hear there has been some trouble. What happened?' Thus without being charged the servant is able to give, at length if he likes, his side of the case. The result is that when both sides have been stated and a judgment made, the boss is able to say either 'You were wrong' and give the required reprimand, with reasons, or 'You were right, but . . .' and explain how the situation should and could have been dealt with so that only an unreasonable guest (whose existence the management is ready to acknowledge) could have lodged a formal complaint.

With young servants, the reprimand administered with justice and some psychological finesse usually works. But it is more difficult with the older men. 'When a man is over thirty—possibly forty or fifty—how can *I* start to bring him up?' asks M. Zembrzuski plaintively.

CHAPTER TEN

FOOD AND WINE

ONLY FIVE restaurants in Paris are honoured with the supreme gastronomic accolade of three stars in the *Guide Michelin*, and none of them is in an hotel. Only three hotels combine the top rating for luxury in general and two stars for cuisine: the Ritz, the George V, and the Plaza Athénée. This guide-book grading, which places the Ritz restaurants one notch below Lasserre, Le Grand Vefour, Lapérouse, Maxim's and the Tour d'Argent, does not in the least disturb the Ritz management, who look with something less than reverence on the *Michelin* judgments anyhow.

The fact that no *hotel* is rated higher than the Ritz on any score enables them to avoid the suspicion of special pleading when they suggest that perhaps the *Michelin* has a tendency to favour the non-hotel restaurant on the ground that hotels are not solely dedicated to gastronomy and therefore not to be considered on quite the same plane as the specialists who do nothing else but cook and serve food.

The Ritz will accept, or at least tolerate, this attitude from experts but it is often expressed by less knowledgeable people, and the kind of glib generalisation which does irk the Ritz is such as appears in one international encyclopaedia of cookery, of British origin, where the author or compiler in her introduction says, 'The meals I have eaten abroad and which have left the most abiding memory . . . are not the grand hotel meals, which are much the same the world over.'

[173]

Another important factor in making comparisons between hotel and restaurant eating is the question of volume; the Ritz has an annual food-and-drink turnover of more than £350,000, which is many times greater than most restaurants, and this means that catering is on a totally different scale.

The Ritz philosophy about food, which is to say the principles and standards evolved by César Ritz and Escoffier, is not that of the non-hotel restaurants, which usually have one or more 'speciality' dishes for which they are celebrated. When Art Buchwald was engaged on the field-work for his *Paris After Dark* he asked a Ritz *maître d'hôtel* what the specialities were. Buchwald records that he 'drew himself up and replied, "The Ritz has no specialities, monsieur, because in a restaurant like the Ritz everything is impeccable."'

'Simplicity, quality and concern for the health of the customer' is the basis of the Ritz creed of cuisine. 'Simplicity' in this context means that the best raw materials shall be used and prepared in such a way that the quality will emerge unmistakably. The corollary of this is a hatred of decoration for decoration's sake. Charles Ritz once made the analogy that beautiful jewels are always at their best in a simple setting. He also made the rather surprisingly worded statement: 'We use simple facts, good logic, and everything is edible'. 'Logic'—a favourite word of his father's here means that it is logical if a customer orders, say, *cervelle*, to ensure that he gets, cooked and served in the best possible way, what is recognisably and indisputably *cervelle*. By 'everything is edible' M. Ritz simply meant that nothing is put before the customer merely because it embellishes or makes the dish prettier. 'Disguise' is another word M. Ritz is apt to use scornfully about over-elaborate presentation; his belief in 'eye-appeal' is strictly confined to the ingredients themselves. 'Never complicate' was one of Escoffier's maxims.

Another example of the Ritz insistence that the attractive must also be functional is the use of well-designed silverware serving-dishes, originally suggested by Escoffier because of the heat-retaining qualities of the metal; Escoffier believed that food being served really hot added twenty-five per cent to its virtue.

Escoffier invented a great many dishes at the Ritz, but there has never been any attempt to suggest that they are exclusive; indeed the measure of their success is that their names have passed into international bill-of-fare language. The Ritz does not, for instance, put any stress on the fact that Pêche Melba originated in its kitchens. Almost any café will offer you Pêche Melba; the Ritz would merely claim that it offers *real* Pêche Melba. The dish has become widely corrupted because it is so easy; every kitchen has ice-cream, tinned peaches and a bottle of syrup. What Escoffier created was rather different. It came about when Dame Nellie Melba was anxious about her figure and could not decide whether to have ice-cream or peaches (she should probably have had neither) at a dinner she was planning. Escoffier said, in effect, why not have both at once? On the basis of fresh peaches and ice-cream he built a dish of fresh *framboises*, a syrup he had made himself, and a finishing touch of diced almonds.

*   *   *

There is a story, probably true, of a man who asked a millionaire how much it cost to run a yacht. 'If you want to know how much it costs, you can't afford a yacht,' the millionaire replied. It is not necessary to be a millionaire to eat at the Ritz, but perhaps it could fairly be said that if you are too much concerned about the prices on the menu you shouldn't be eating there at all. However, the plain fact is that the Ritz restaurants are by no means the most expensive in Paris, far less in the world; not only is it possible to pay far more for a meal in New York, but the Ritz has nothing to compare with the £2 steak, the thirty-shilling hamburger or the four-and-sixpenny cup of coffee reported by reliable witnesses from Los Angeles.

The Ritz bills of fare are relatively short and simple—and, incidentally, easily manageable manually, which is more than can be said of many restaurants. A specimen dinner menu of the restaurant lists four soups, nine fish dishes, nine entrées, three roasts (these classically simple: chicken, saddle of lamb, partridge), four vegetables and eight sweets. There are also the standard uncategorised items—smoked salmon, caviare, smoked ham and *foie gras*. The most expensive item on the menu is caviare at 52s. The entrées average about a guinea. A notable concession to the trend of the times is the suggested short dinner ('for instant service') which provides three courses—three pairs of alternatives: soup; fish or chicken; and sweet—for 36s. There is a cover-and-butter charge of 6s. and the compulsory minimum for a meal without drink is 30s. In other words, dinner at the Ritz, with an apéritif and a bottle of wine for two, is likely to cost about seven pounds.

Not only the *plats du jour* but all the other dishes are changed every day.

The grill-room has a slightly longer *carte*. A luncheon menu taken as a random example shows three *plats du jour*—trout, sole and turkey. The inclusive lunch (again 36s.) is in this case *hors d'œuvres* or soup; sole or turkey; and a sweet. Aside from the ubiquitously costly caviare, the most expensive dish is *poulet à l'anglaise* at 30s. A Chateaubriand for two is 48s.

I have, of course, omitted for simplicity the descriptions of how the dishes are cooked. What I have called baldly 'turkey' is in fact *Dindonneau poêlé aux chipolatas et bacon, velouté de marrons*'; my 'trout' is '*truite de vivier au beurre nantais*'. And I have not attempted to render, except as 'entrée' such a euphonious dish as '*cœur de charolais Marigny*'.

The records show that the average bill per person for dinner at the Ritz is £3 and at lunch £2 10s. (For comparison, I looked back half a century in the records. The averages then were £1 1s. for dinner and 10s. for lunch.)

* * *

As in so many other departments of the Ritz, there is a strong line of continuity between the *maîtres d'hôtel* of the restaurant. The present holder of the office, Robert Sénéchal, was a *commis* under the great Olivier and five years ago he took over from Olivier's successor, Michel. Sénéchal is a young-looking fifty-nine, despite the fact that he spent five years of the Second World War as a prisoner of war in Germany. 'A wasteful time,' he says now, with a smile. 'There was little opportunity to develop in one's métier.'

Sénéchal came to the Ritz as a boy in 1919 and after three years went to London for a time and worked at the Café Royal to gain experience and to improve his English.

By the 'great days' of the Twenties, the boom years between war and slump, he was a full-fledged waiter. The highlight of his recollections in general is the famous Sunday night gala dinners. One of those splendid occasions provided a moment about which he laughs now but at the time regarded as the most dreadful thing that had ever happened to him professionally.

At a table of which he was in charge there was a lady in a resplendent red velvet coat, which she had thrown back from her bare shoulders. One of Sénéchal's *commis* was carrying a large dish of strawberry Melba between tables when Sénéchal, from some distance away, saw the *commis* being accidentally jostled and momentarily losing his balance. The dish tipped and Sénéchal, staring in horror and unable to prevent disaster, watched the whole strawberry Melba slide off the dish and disappear between the coat and the bare back. The woman did not start or jump or scream. She simply froze, with an expression of absolute incredulity on her face. Nothing similar has ever happened since, but Sénéchal still touches wood when he says this, for of such incidents are a waiter's nightmares composed.

Sénéchal's memories are vivid and varied. He recalls with rapture the beauty and shy charm of Princess Marina in her teens; there was one particular charity ball for émigré Russians in Paris which she attended every year and it is evident that, though she never knew it, the young princess became what in later, less elegant times would be called his pin-up girl. He recalls the magnificence of parties given for and by Barbara Hutton, particularly the one to celebrate her first wedding anniversary, when the restaurant was transformed into a Moroccan bazaar.

He has, of course, had his share of memorable oddities and eccentrics, like the rich American woman who insisted on raw cabbage salad at every meal and as an apéritif drank a glass of vinegar with a spoonful of sugar in it. Sénéchal still shudders at the thought. And there was the man whose fad was to drink nothing but donkey milk, which the wine butler had to serve. One day it had fermented in the bottle and when it was opened it exploded over everybody for yards around. As the guest supplied his own donkey milk there was no one to blame but himself.

For a boy coming to the Ritz when Sénéchal did there were some curious sights. It was the time of the maharajahs who brought their own cooks and would eat only the food they prepared. Sénéchal was fascinated by the Maharajah of Bikinir who had a moustache spoon (along the lines of a moustache cup, with a built-in strainer) and the Maharajah of Patiala, who used to carry a piece of string with which to tie back his beard and keep it out of his food. But like all good hotel men Sénéchal has gained by every experience. 'We make very good curries here, you know,' Sénéchal says. 'After all, we had the very best teachers.'

It is, of course, common knowledge that we eat less than our forebears—even than our fathers. When Sénéchal was a waiter no dinner was complete without two meat courses and usually a sherbet was served in the middle of the meal. He accepts the shorter, simpler meals of today, but he confessed to a kind of nostalgia when he recently served a dinner given to celebrate a golden wedding. The host and hostess wanted to have the sort of dinner they were accustomed to as a celebration when they were first married. They omitted the sherbet and included salad (which they would not have done fifty years ago), but what they did order was on a scale which is rarely encountered now and at which even an expense account business man might blench. Without giving the detailed names of each course, here is what the dinner consisted of:

Caviare	Salad
Lobster (cold)	Cheese
Chicken in mushrooms	Ice Cream
Kid	Fruit
Foie gras	

Sénéchal follows the *maître d'hôtel* tradition of buying all his own fruit, every day in summer when the soft fruits require special care and at least twice a week the rest of the year. He does this on his way to work in the morning. He is proud of never serving a melon he has not personally selected and regards anybody who buys such fruit by the case—a common practice in catering—as a lunatic, or worse.

*　　*　　*

The *maître d'hôtel* of the grill-room, L'Espadon, is, like his other-side-of-the-house colleague, Sénéchal, in the modern line of holders of this office, neither obsequious nor majestic but anxious to please and unobtrusively helpful and charming. He is also youthful-looking though in the late fifties, and quietist in his approach to his job. He is a handsome, silver-haired man known as Paul, but many Ritz regulars could not tell you whether that is his first name or surname. In fact, he was born André Paul and he started as a part-time waiter (lunch only) in the old grill-room in 1936. He has been in charge of L'Espadon since it opened and, as every *maître d'hôtel* puts his stamp, blatantly or subtly, on his restaurant, he must be credited with a considerable degree of the success of that rarity, a first-class Paris restaurant which has established itself firmly in a few years.

Before his present job, Paul was what Charles Ritz teasingly describes in his presence as 'the beau of the *thé*'—meaning that when afternoon tea at the Ritz was an important and fashionable institution of Paris life Paul was the man about whom it all revolved; who gave '*le* five o'clock' its tone and distinction. With his good looks and soft voice, somewhat like an actor of the Charles Boyer school, it is easy to understand. 'Half the ladies would not move beyond the doorway of the salon until Paul had greeted and "seated" them personally,' says M. Ritz.

But Paul modestly says that the real king of the *salon de thé* was his predecessor, George Elles (brother of the manager Elles), whose deputy Paul was. Elles presided over the salon before the war, the peak days of '*le* five o'clock'; Paul took over after the Liberation and enjoyed a full decade in charge. But since about

[179]

1955 there has been a decline, or perhaps a shift in social habits would be a better description, and although the salon still functions busily in the late afternoon it is not the social imperative it once was. It is noticeable that the cocktail glass occasionally replaces the teacup and there is not the same fastidious selection of ices and éclairs; the age of the habitués tends to be older and Paul explains that this is inevitable, as the younger generation, even of the aristocracy, takes life more seriously, from necessity if not from choice. They work for their living or they are students, in which case they are more likely to be found in St German des Prés or in some brasserie.

L'Espadon's notable success is in having attracted Parisians who are inclined, as a generalisation, to stay away from hotel restaurants and to prefer their favourite bistros or 'specialist' restaurants solely devoted to food. At first, often through being entertained at L'Espadon by foreign friends, they were surprised to discover the range of the cuisine, though Paul adheres to the classic simplicity of Escoffier and the grill-room puts its emphasis on sea-food and grills. The new décor, too, they found attractive, intimate and unlike the usual conception of a restaurant within an hotel.

Yet there were difficulties to be overcome. Foreign visitors may either be staying in the hotel or moving around in taxis, but the native Parisian with his own car finds parking in central Paris extremely difficult. Then the fashion houses, which used to be good customers of the grill-room, have tended to move away from the Place Vendôme area towards the streets around the Champs Elysées. (Mme Chanel in the Rue Cambon is the notable exception.)

An easily overlooked factor is the effect television has had on French social life. The single channel available in Paris is more generally, and on the whole more sharply, criticised or abused than even the television services of England or America, but there is no doubt that because of it people stay at home more. Paul has customers who admit that because of television they dine out at a restaurant now only once a week whereas they used to do so two or three times. They have perhaps four restaurants they like and the result is that Paul, who used to see them regularly at least once a week, now sees them once a month.

Among non-Parisian visitors, Paul reckons on about forty regulars who spend some time in Paris every year. There is, of course, a much larger number of 'occasionals' and Paul likes to surprise them by recognising their voices on the telephone, perhaps after an absence of several years. He has two Princesses Aga Khan, for instance—the widow and the second wife of the late Aga Khan—but he never confuses them, as he knows which it is by the voice.

The Duke and Duchess of Windsor are occasional but faithful customers. One small problem, typical of what will worry a devoted head waiter, troubled Paul for a time in connection with them. The Duke has a favourite whisky, and when he asked for it Paul could never make out the name. He would say '*Pardon?*' but after two attempts he would give up and say he regretted they did not have that brand. He worried, because if only he could get hold of the name he would ensure that the whisky was obtained, even if nobody else ever asked for it. His patience was rewarded at last; by roundabout means he discovered that what the Duke was saying, in his English voice, was two letters the English sounds of which are unknown in French—'J. & B.'*

The late Aly Khan was a regular, with the idiosyncrasy that he liked to come and have sherbets all alone in the afternoon. Paul cherishes (or cherished) the patronage of Greta Garbo, Rita Hayworth, the Humphrey Bogarts, Douglas Fairbanks and Mary Pickford, Cary Grant, and Charlie Chaplin, and he remembers (partly because he was so shocked at the time) William Boyd giving away Hopalong Cassidy medals with his portrait on them.

Again like Sénéchal, Paul finds that people eat less now and that meals are shorter and simpler, even the dinner parties ordered in advance. He approves of the two- or three-course dinner which is well chosen, and offered me examples which were

* "J. & B. Rare"—the blend popularised in recent years, especially in America, by the London firm of Justerini & Brooks.

to be served soon after we talked. One consisted of *loup flambé* followed by turkey; the other, scampi *gratinés* followed by saddle of lamb. Some of the guests would probably have a sweet, but Paul says he is virtually never asked for savouries now, though they used to be the rule. Cheese and salad have taken their place in popularity.

The last of the 'big entertaining' in Paul's life went out with Mrs James Corrigan, the celebrated American hostess, but he was reminded of the old days recently when an elderly celebration party ordered oysters, fish, poultry, meat, *foie gras*, cheese and dessert.

A favourite character in Paul's Ritz memories is a waiter known as Ginger, who worked at the hotel from the age of sixteen until he was seventy-two. When Ginger was a *commis* he was given the daily task of delivering two eggs to a woman who had moved out of the hotel to an apartment of her own. She had an obsession about the freshness of eggs and thought only Olivier could be trusted to supply them. For a while Ginger made this excursion every morning as soon as he came on duty, but eventually he figured that he could have an hour longer in bed if he took the eggs home with him at night and delivered them on his way to work. The only trouble was that the eggs were stamped with the date, but Ginger got round this difficulty by getting hold of the stamp at night and moving it one digit forward. But one night he slipped up on this. Next day the woman telephoned Olivier in distress and said, 'What shall I do? You've sent me tomorrow's eggs.' Naturally Olivier said he would send two more round for today, but that was the end of Ginger's little game.

Ginger liked jokes, but sometimes they misfired. An American steel magnate's wife once found that the staff at her château had been drinking the wine from her cellar in her absence. She was worried about the quality of what was left and, having no knowledge herself, brought a sample bottle to the Ritz for identification. She showed it to Ginger, saying, 'I suppose this is all right, but I'd like to be sure.' Ginger pointed to the boldly monogrammed 'N' on the bottle and said solemnly, 'Madame, you have a treasure there—the wine of Napoleon.' In fact the 'N' stood for Nicolas, a popular chain of wineshops. The lady was so impressed that she took the bottle to the management and asked that it should be put in the hotel safe. Some time later she had it served at lunch and found it was a very ordinary, inexpensive *vin rouge*. She immediately complained that somebody had switched the contents with another bottle, as this could not be 'the wine of Napoleon'. The manager, Elmiger, had to tell her the truth—but it cost the hotel a good bottle of wine to console her. And Ginger was in trouble again.

* * *

The success of L'Espadon, its recognition by experts as a new restaurant of distinction, is a proud achievement for the Ritz, and for Paul. A famous restaurant *within* a famous hotel is notoriously rare. 'The exalted demands of gastronomy,' wrote Joseph Wechsberg in *Esquire* not long ago, 'make it impossible for the average hotel manager to run a great restaurant, so to speak, as a side-line; only a great restaurateur or chef can do that. But the Ritz has come back into the epicurean *cercle privé* of Paris. When I was there a while ago two great experts (both of them own famous restaurants in Paris themselves) told me about the comeback of the Ritz. And an honoured member of that fastidious gathering of gastronomes, the Club des Cents . . . told me with an air of finality, "You can eat well now at the grill-room of the Ritz . . . everybody goes there nowadays."'

* * *

The definition of the function of a *sommelier*, or even a head wine-waiter, varies greatly. He can be anything from a man who recommends the wines on his list according to price, snobbery, his own taste, what he thinks the customer rates or will stand for (or indeed what the cellar wants to unload) to a connoisseur who lives and dreams wine and whose responsibility extends to tending a fine cellar and buying judiciously for its constant replenishment. In the second category he earns the nobler title of *chef des caves*, and his most important work is done out of sight of the customers.

[183]

There have been only two *chefs des caves* at the Ritz since it opened. The original, Guichard, was in charge when the present incumbent, Maurice, arrived in 1929. Maurice, who took over three years later, is a gentle, frail little man in his late sixties who has been seriously ill. This is a worry to the management, firstly because he is beloved by all, but also because there is no obvious successor to his highly skilled job.

To walk through his cellars with Maurice and listen to him is to realise his dedication to the art and science of *œnologie* and his pride in the quality of the Ritz storehouse of wines. The stock, divided between the hotel vaults and the longer-term storage in the Rue Lecourbe, now comprises some 80,000 bottles. It was once 150,000 bottles, but the run-down is deliberate as the turnover in wines is quicker than it used to be, and Maurice will eventually reduce his stock to about 60,000 bottles. Younger wines are being drunk now and there is not the same need to have large stocks of maturing wines. This also means that less capital is tied up in the cellars.

Maurice gives all the credit to Guichard for laying the foundations of the Ritz cellars, which, he will assure you, are second to none in the world today. Guichard left treasures for those who would come after him, and Maurice has simply tried to continue the good work.

Maurice's real name is Boris Guyot, but '*Boreece*' was soon Gallicised into '*Maureece*', and Maurice he has remained. He is a greengrocer's son from a village in Seine-et-Oise. The greengrocer also sold wine and Maurice learned the rudiments in his father's shop. At fifteen he came to Paris. In those days there was no 'hotel school', so the ambitious student worked for his living in the mornings and evenings, and studied in the afternoons. There was, however, a celebrated wine expert, M. Hoop, who was prepared to instruct young seekers after knowledge at his apartment in the Rue Richelieu. Later, in his time off, Maurice studied under Professor Brunet—'he wrote a *beautiful* book about wine' —and he still speaks with veneration about his tutors.

Meanwhile he worked as a junior wine waiter at the Continental and other hotels and at the Cercle Interallié, the venue of many important receptions, especially diplomatic, and there he gained valuable experience. There also he met M. Garros, an agent for Bordeaux wines, who specialised in supplying the embassies and high society. Garros told the boy that to get on he must know English, so Maurice went to London and lived in Hornsey for eight months.

After serving in the First World War he went back to the Cercle Interallié, and then to the Ritz.

The vital responsibility of a *chef des caves* is, of course, buying wine and in this Guichard was Maurice's final teacher. But Maurice also applied himself to educating the *sommeliers* who, in his opinion, were not as knowledgeable as they ought to be with such fine cellars at their disposal. One reason for their short-comings was that in those days almost everybody who dined or entertained at the Ritz was a connoisseur of claret and knew precisely what he wanted. If a customer ordered a Château Margaux, Château Latour or a Cheval Blanc of a certain year the *sommelier* was quite at home; but if somebody asked to be more generally recommended to a good Pauillac or St Julien or St Estèphe the waiter was not so reliable. By the time Maurice was in charge of the cellars he felt the customers were being guided properly to what they ought to drink.

Although tastes have changed in Maurice's thirty-odd years at the Ritz one thing has remained curiously constant: the proportion of clarets to Burgundies sold is roughly four to one. The biggest change has been since the last war and it is a decrease in the veneration of age in wines. Maurice does not mind this; too much respect can be paid to age and many wines are rewarding drunk younger than used to be thought right. This is especially true of champagne; less of it is drunk now, and so long as there are champagnes of the best years back to 1952 Maurice is content.

The decline in champagne-drinking among the French has been marked in recent years, to the despair of M. Auzello, and it has been matched by the growth of a taste (and a fashion) for Scotch whisky. At a reception where once a hundred bottles of champagne would have been served there will now be only fifty; the rest is whisky. Maurice shrugs and smiles: 'It is less trouble, it is just as profitable for the hotel; the only person it is not good for is the champagne agent.'

The secret of wine-buying is to select wines which your customers will want in years to come, and which will not be, by then, ruinously expensive. Of course, prices are rising steadily; in 1914 a bottle of vintage champagne at the Ritz cost on average the equivalent of 9s. 6d. Today the average is £2 10s. and though the prices go up to £4 a bottle this still makes it relatively modest compared with the night-club which charges £5 a bottle with no credentials as to quality.

But a more illustrative comparison is that in 1953 and 1955 Maurice bought fine clarets at 1,200 old francs a bottle (say 18s.). The 1959 clarets of approximately the same quality should have cost about 1,500 to sell at comparable prices. But in fact they cost 2,200—and the 1961s went up to 2,800, and will have to be sold at more than double. By the time these wines are ready to drink, Maurice wonders, will people have become accustomed to paying that much for the wine they want? That is the gamble that has to be taken in buying wine for the future.

Once a year M. Auzello conducts a wine-tasting, with Maurice, which goes on for a week and on which the year's buying is decided. This is a solemn occasion, full of delicacy and hazard. 'It is not easy,' M. Auzello says, 'to decide in May on the quality of the previous year's vintage. Sometimes'—he grimaced expressively—'we are drinking vinegar. One has to guess how it will turn out.'

Once the selections are made, the Ritz then has, as Auzello says, to 'pay the board' of the chosen wines for three or four years at the vineyard before it is bottled. They buy the wine outright and do not simply take options. When the wine is bottled, samples are sent to the buyer and that is an anxious moment. Now the decision is whether to increase the order or to sell the wine, according to how, in their opinion, it has developed. After bottling and delivery, the wine will remain two or three years in the cellar without appearing on the wine-list—and even then, says Auzello, 'you still don't know if the *customers* will like it'.

Experts like Auzello and Maurice talk of wine as a living thing, which in a sense it is; it 'works' (as they say) all the time until it is drunk. 'Nature,' says Auzello sadly, 'does not always follow the experts' expectations. Often a wine does not live up to its promise.' Every week Auzello and Maurice taste some bottles to see how various wines are shaping. 'Usually the wine that is going to turn out best matures slowly,' Auzello told me, 'but some are found to be "galloping", others "trotting".' The analogy with horse-racing is not far-fetched. It is frequently found that wine A is away out ahead at one tasting, by the next time round wine B has overtaken it, and then along comes wine C and leaves both the others behind.

So far the Ritz has bought only first to fifth *crus* (growths), but in future they realise they will have to buy lower *crus* because they feel they must always be able to offer a reasonable bottle of claret at between £1 and £2 in the list, and in the higher grades this will not be possible in years to come. 'There are occasional bargains in buying wine,' Maurice said—'not many; and of course the worst bargain is the wine you can't sell.'

One day when I was with Maurice in the cellars I was perched on a stool in his tiny office, stacked with wine merchants' lists. The telephone rang. The bell is geared to be heard by the cellar-men wherever they are and the blast by my ear nearly knocked me off my stool. There followed a long, earnest conversation between Maurice and Sénéchal, the restaurant *maître d'hôtel* upstairs. I thought I followed the gist of it, but when Maurice came off the telephone I asked him if, forgiving my curiosity, he would confirm that I had heard what I thought I had. He did so. The point was that on the wine-list there is a 1924 Château d'Yquem at 25 NF a bottle and a 1953 at 40 NF. Maurice has no doubt that the older and cheaper is the better wine, and the discussion had been as to which should be served at a certain forthcoming reception. The real issue was whether the hosts were the sort of people who would appreciate the 25-franc wine or the sort who would prefer the 40-franc, assuming the dearer to be the better. The discussion ended with the decision that the party-givers were worthy of the compliment of being served the cheaper wine.

That settled, Maurice returned to the general picture. His
stock approximates two-thirds red wine to one-third white. This
represents a slight reduction in the demand for white wine over
the years, but among the white wines themselves there has been a
dramatic change in taste. People have moved so solidly towards
dry wines that nowadays eighty per cent of the white wine sold is
white Burgundy and only two per cent white Bordeaux. (The
remaining eighteen per cent comprises *champagne nature*, Rhine,
Moselle and Alsatian wines.)

Maurice has one grievance against the wine-makers. Before
the war, sixty per cent of high-quality French wine was sold in
France. Now wine is being drunk much more widely abroad and
the export market is booming. Maurice claims that the vineyards
are deliberately selling less in the domestic market, as they can
sell up to eighty per cent of their product at higher prices abroad.
'They will now only let us have enough for us to act as their
ambassadors,' he said disgruntledly. 'Each year more and more
visitors drink French wine and so they want it when they get
home. We are in effect the salesmen, but it does *us* no good.'

We made a tour of another part of the cellar, Maurice com-
menting lovingly on what we passed. 'Ah,' he said, pointing to
some racks bearing a dusty label to the effect that here was once
the private reserve of Calouste Gulbenkian, who lived in the
hotel. 'Mainly 1926 clarets. When they were new nobody thought
they were going to be particularly good, but Mr Gulbenkian was
certain—and he proved to be right.'

At a crossroads among the racks Maurice suddenly pulled my
sleeve. Carefully he lifted down a magnum and showed it to me
with pride. It was a Château Mouton-Rothschild 1952; he has
only a few—some Château Lafite and Château Latour as well—
all of which are now virtually unobtainable in magnum. Next he
climbed a ladder to the top of a rack and tenderly brought down
a bottle of Richebourg 1906. 'Not too old?' I asked. Maurice held
the bottle up to the light so that I could admire the clarity. Then
he pointed to the space separating the cork and the top of the
wine; it was no more than half an inch. 'You see?' he said. 'You
can tell it is in good condition without opening it. You can tell

much by just looking. It is no use having an old wine if you have to open ten bottles to find a good one.'

He returned to the bottle in his hand. 'You see, the colour is good. No air has entered since it was bottled. This will not be a strong wine—rather thin, but interesting as a curiosity and its condition is a tribute to the cellar. To be able to keep wines well over a long time is the most important quality in a cellar. One, of course, must not be too academic. Wine is for drinking and the cellar is not a museum. To have this bottle is interesting, but in buying today one must not be bound too much by old standards. For example, by the old rules we should be selling 1955 white Burgundy now, whereas in fact we are selling 1959, and it is very good indeed.' (Auzello too does not disapprove of the modern taste for young white wines; the former insistence on greater age, he says, was merely *snobisme*.)

Maurice, however, has his criticisms of modern tastes. 'I have wines here,' he said severely, 'that I would rather say were finished than see served to people who are talking and drinking cocktails.'

There was little evidence in the cellars of the cobwebs so often taken as evidence of great age in wines. I asked if cobwebs had ever signified anything. 'Oh, yes,' said Maurice quickly. 'There is a fly which lays eggs which produce worms which eat through corks. We used to cultivate spiders' webs because they caught the flies. It is not necessary now because we have insecticides.'

Although Maurice does not sigh for the past he does find people now in rather too much of a hurry. 'They used to have time to ask about wine—to improve their knowledge,' he said. 'You had to explain sometimes, for example, that Fine Champagne has nothing to do with champagne but is so called because it is brandy made in a particular small area of Cognac. Now few people have time to ask, so they don't learn so much.' He added, also regretfully, that it is rarely possible nowadays to decant wine some hours before serving, as few people order until they are at the table. Both Auzello and Maurice enjoy catering for banquets or private parties where the food and wine are decided well in advance and there is plenty of time to have the wine decanted and *chambré.* 'It is only in this way,' Auzello says, 'that the true connoisseur can appreciate a really fine wine.'

*   *   *

Maurice is concerned about the future of cellar experts and wine waiters; there is not enough training of young people, he says, and also perhaps fewer young people who want to study and be trained. A pet project of his is to have a room in the hotel to which young members of the staff could go in their time off. It would have books on food and wine. ('There are good documentary films about wine too.') He would also have gramophone language-lessons, using earphones. There would be no compulsion on staff to use this room, but doing so would be taken as a sign of keenness to learn; when the chance arose for promotion or to send a boy to England (always a step on the way to the top) one who had done some studying would be preferred.

*   *   *

The Ritz approach to any new departure in its business is inevitably wary, discreet and dignified, but once the decision is made the management can be at least as smart as any younger and brasher business in its exploitation. A few years ago M. Auzello decided that there was one trend of the times in catering that should be followed. Explaining his thinking to me, he said, 'In this changing world the individual is not enough to provide a lunching and dining clientele. The leisured rich are scarce; the big executive is the new class and so one has to develop a new line of business. The best way for executives to meet and to entertain is round a good table, in the proper atmosphere.' The words 'expense account' were never mentioned, but that was the trade Auzello had in mind. The result is that the Ritz now does a big business in private parties, banquets and (that wide-embracing French word) 'receptions'.

Auzello's first action was to write some five hundred words of elegant prose. (He submitted them to a literary friend for approval and was delighted to have to make no amendments.) He then had a brochure of matching elegance designed and printed and sent one to each of a hundred carefully chosen executives, such as heads of banks and big businesses. Characteristically, he included a few apt lines from Montaigne's Essays which he remembered: 'Keeping a good table requires no little skill and devotion. Not even the great generals or the great philosophers disdained the use and science of the table.'

After a paragraph or two about the traditions of the Ritz, invoking the great names of César and Escoffier, Auzello wrote: 'Sometimes to defend a tradition is to ignore progress' and proceeded gently to discourse on post-war changes in the life of all of us which called for 'a new orientation'. This softest of selling eventually reached the hard fact that the Ritz could provide, in private rooms, anything from dinners and lunches to cocktail parties (*cinq à sept, avec buffet*), wedding receptions, betrothal parties and *bals privés* for up to 1,200 guests. Always sensitive to atmosphere, the Ritz makes a point of its having no formal 'banqueting rooms' but simply private rooms of varying sizes; there are echoes here of the founder's idea of his hotel being like your own home, provided you had the money and the taste to have such a home.

Apart from the prosperous commerce of these functions which the Ritz now frequently houses, there is the pleasure for Auzello and company of having menus and wines chosen in advance, which they believe improves them greatly. Some organisations which meet at the Ritz, such as the gastronomic Club des Cents, have a 'rehearsal' luncheon at which Auzello, with a few officials of the club, offers and discusses what he suggests the food and drink should be. Not long ago the president of such a club complained that the inclusive price suggested was too high. Auzello said that if the best is to be provided it costs what it costs. But nevertheless, he said, a reduction might be made if a less expensive white wine were to be served with the fish course. For the rehearsal lunch Auzello had Maurice serve three white wines, two being those he had originally budgeted for and one the Macon *blanc* which was currently the cheapest on the list but which Auzello thought particularly good. The labels of all the bottles were covered up. The experts tasted, considered, and

voted unanimously for the Macon *blanc*. Auzello then informed
them that he could now reduce the price per head by nine
shillings. At the dinner the wine was served decanted and only
one guest in this company of connoisseurs recognised it for what
it was. He did not object to it—he simply knew it. 'He was a
Senator from Marseille—Provençal, like me,' Auzello added,
chuckling with chauvinistic pride.

*   *   *

There are two specialists at the Ritz who deserve a footnote.
First, Jean Combet, a waiter in L'Espadon, who is responsible
for the buying of all the hotel's cheese and is also the acknowledged and peerless master of *crêpes Suzette*.

It is probably in the tradition of Escoffier that while *crêpes
Suzette*, almost above any other dish, is the subject of endless
controversy as to method and content and, in many places, of
absurdly overdone ceremony, Combet regards it as all perfectly
simple. He cooks it and serves it with speed and a minimum of
fuss. Ask why he should be the acknowledged master of this art
and you will be answered with a shrug; it is simply that Combet's
crêpes Suzette are the best.

Combet has been at the Ritz for twenty-five years and is the
unusual combination of cook turned waiter. He learned his
crêpes Suzette making when he was at the Ambassador at Cannes
where the *maître d'hôtel*, Mancini, was, he says, the greatest
crêpes man in the world.

Far from guarding secrets, Combet is eager to tell how to make
crêpes Suzette properly. Small quantities are the root of the
matter. A very little butter on the dish, very small shavings of
orange peel, a little Grand Marnier, a little caramel sauce, a
little orange juice. When these and the dish are very hot, put on
the pancake; after a moment, turn it (still flat), then add a
noisette of fresh butter, a little sprinkle of sugar, a little lemon
juice. Then fold the pancake over, add a little Cusenier *extra sec*
orange liqueur, a touch more sugar, a little squeeze of lemon
and then *flamber* with brandy.*

    * Combet, it will be noticed, starts with the pancake ready-made, and most
recipes for *crêpes Suzette* do the same. This is, of course, a very professional

It seems to be impossible to establish dogmatically who invented *crêpes Suzette*, in what circumstances, and who Suzette was. One of the most popular stories is that Escoffier created the dish especially for Edward VII (then Prince of Wales). The Prince asked what it was called and Escoffier said it had no name yet. He asked the Prince for a suggestion and, it is said, the Prince named it after his dinner companion—which, of course, still leaves us with the question, who was Suzette? It has to be added that the same story has also been attributed to another famous chef, Charpentier.

The Prince's admiration for Ritz and Escoffier, and the frequency with which he was their patron, suggests Escoffier as the more likely candidate, but it is curious that when Mme Ritz wrote about the fact that many of Escoffier's most famous creations were named after women—Isabelle, Hélène, Eve, Solange, Georgette, Alice, Cecilia, Rosemonde, Dora—she did not include Suzette.

Combet's knowledge of cheese began in the kitchens. When L'Espadon opened it was decided to make a speciality of cheese and Combet was put in charge of the buying. He uses only two shops, in the Madeleine area, and goes there once a week.

His basic purchases are of the classic French cheese—said to be the most difficult to buy skilfully—Camembert and Brie. Next come Roquefort, Reblochon (from Savoie), Châteaubriand (a cream cheese from Normandy) and Pont l'Evèque. He buys no foreign cheese except Dutch, and not much of that. He is

---

approach, where the quality of the pancake can be taken for granted. Escoffier, however, in his *Guide to Modern Cookery* (Heinemann, 1920), gives details of his preparation for the pancake: Take 1 lb. flour in basin, 6 oz. powdered sugar, pinch of salt. Dilute with ten eggs and one quart of milk, added by degrees. Flavour with one heaped tablespoonful of orange, lemon or vanilla sugar, which should form part of the total weight of sugar prescribed, or with one-eighth of a pint of some liqueur such as brandy, kirsch, rum, etc., which should form part of the total moistening. When the pancake is intended for *crêpes Suzette*, he adds, it should be flavoured with curaçao and tangerine juice and coated with softened butter similarly flavoured.

well aware that there are excellent English cheeses but he has no demand for them.

The other off-beat specialist of the Ritz is called Trinquier. He is a quiet, earnest-looking elderly man, usually seen wearing the blue jeans and denim jacket of a porter. He goes in and out of the hotel on a variety of errands and his commissions are mainly executed by bicycle. But what gives Trinquier his special distinction is that he is the oyster-buyer for the Ritz. He has the reputation of having an unequalled eye (or is it nose or finger?) for the best oysters. He never buys a large quantity from any one place. He bustles around tirelessly, examining what is on offer, buying two dozen here, three dozen there, until he has the required quantity.

Trinquier came to the Ritz in an odd way. He was a soldier at Nîmes when Auzello was there in 1940, but they met only once and Auzello did not even know his name. Trinquier was operating the telephone switchboard at the headquarters of Auzello's commanding officer. After Auzello was back at the Ritz later that year he was told one day that a man named Trinquier wished to see him. The name meant nothing, but when the caller was shown in he recognised the telephone operator.

Trinquier was looking for a job. As what? Auzello asked. Trinquier said he had once been a waiter, but his qualifications were not up to Ritz requirements, and Auzello said there was nothing he could offer. A moment after Trinquier had left the room Auzello had an idea. He was at that time buying supplies for the hotel wherever he could find them, often in small quantities in outlying places. He jumped up and called after the departing job-hunter. 'Have you a bicycle?' he asked. (Bicycles were then at a premium in Paris.) Trinquier sadly said no. 'Ah,' said Auzello, 'then it is no use.' 'But I can have one by tomorrow,' said Trinquier. Auzello admired his willingness and confidence, and the fact that he did not waste time asking questions. Next day he returned with the bicycle and he has been working for Auzello ever since. 'It was thanks to him that this hotel was fed during the occupation,' Auzello assured me. Trinquier got into and out of a lot of trouble (he was questioned, imprisoned, and beaten up on various occasions by inquisitive Germans), but he never either complained nor said whom he represented. ('Trinquier would jump in the fire for M. Auzello,' one Ritz man said to me in admiring awe.)

I once asked for a definition of Trinquier's job. After a moment's hesitation the answer came, with solemn dignity: 'He is M. Auzello's roving ambassador.'

CHAPTER ELEVEN

PART OF THE SERVICE

ONE OF the closest fraternities, or unofficial trade unions, in the world has no formal organisation and its members live and work anything from a few yards to thousands of miles apart; never under the same roof. A fictitious example of the fraternity in action will best illustrate its operation.

A traveller leaves his London hotel without repaying a sum of money, large or small according to the credit rating he enjoys, which he has borrowed from the hall porter in a moment of emergency; perhaps he had nothing but dollars and wanted to pay off a hired car. The oversight is, of course, accidental; the matter has simply slipped his memory. He arrives in Rome. Not at once, but at a suitable moment, the hall porter will mention, very politely, the little matter left unsettled in London. Les Clefs d'Or, the international brotherhood of *concierges*, has, discreetly but effectively, been at work again.

Les Clefs d'Or, named after the insignia of golden keys which every head hall porter wears on the collar of his uniform, bands together for their mutual benefit and protection the major *concierges* of the hotel world. There is much more to it, of course, than simply the collection of *débours*, the disbursements of a hundred different sorts which a *concierge* makes every day for his hotel's clients. Even hotel managers do not know much about the detailed interchanges of intelligence which flow between *concierges*; trust is just as much the essence of the relationship between a *concierge* and his employer as it is between a *concierge* and his clients; and when you trust a man—indeed employ him *because* you trust him—you do not interfere or put your nose too much into the conduct of his affairs.

Nobody has ever seen a *concierge* writing letters or making private long-distance calls. But it is well known that the *concierges* of the principal hotels of the world always know all about each other's business. If your credit is good at, say, Claridge's in London it is likely to be just as good at the Excelsior in Rome, though you may not be personally at all well known to the *concierge* there. In other words, if you are *persona grata* with one major *concierge* it is wise to tell him where you are going next; it is only a matter of leaving a forwarding address, but in effect it is as good as a letter of credit.

A young woman I know was once telephoned from abroad by a somewhat imperious and very rich dowager of her acquaintance and instructed (asked is not the right word) to make a long list of purchases against the older woman's arrival in London. When the Englishwoman, somewhat alarmed at the scale of the shopping list, murmured something about money the dowager simply said, 'Don't be silly. Go to George at the X hotel and get a couple of hundred pounds.'

The London woman was not familiar with the X hotel, as it was considerably above her economic stratum, but she went along, somewhat diffidently explained her mission, and was given the money without a moment's hesitation by a man who to her knowledge had never seen her in his life before and never even asked her name. She does not know to this day whether her rich friend had telephoned or whether the mention of *her* name was enough. She probably underestimates both her honest face and the practised skill of the *concierge* as a character assessor. But the incident is typical of the world of *concierges*.

In another case a foreigner leaving London dumped a skirt on a friend and said, 'I want that changed. Give it to—' naming another *concierge*. The friend never knew who executed the mission, but the *concierge* accepted the parcel without demur and the exchange was duly carried out.

[197]

The *concierge* is therefore anything from an international banker to a universal aunt, and his art is to make everything seem easy and natural. With discretion, of course, as the watchword.

One result of this, almost inevitably, is that *concierges* don't talk. 'The *concierge* sees most of the game,' one senior hotel man said to me, but I have tried to interview them and while I have never been met with anything but charm and courtesy I have never emerged with so much as a paragraph worth printing. I have a feeling that the day one finds a *concierge* who will talk for publication one will have found a bad *concierge*, and therefore I respect their reticence. (The famous Greek-born George of the London Ritz wrote his memoirs, but that was after he retired.)

The *concierge* is the fountain-head of the ancillary services a good hotel provides. He is the answerer of questions, the translator of wish into reality, the fixer supreme. The questions may be simple: Where can I get my hair cut? Which theatre—or restaurant—should I go to? There are restaurants in Paris where the unknown foreigner may not be able to make a short-notice reservation, but miraculously the same demand, routed through Robert, the head *concierge* at the Ritz, will produce a table. (Robert was the Ritz postmaster for some years before 1945, when M. Auzello, who had watched him and decided he was 'quick, precise and indefatigable', appointed him *concierge*.)

And even at the Ritz the *concierge* does not assume that money is no object; he will protect his clients from unnecessary extravagance. I asked one of Robert's deputies to get me a car to take me to the airport and he immediately quoted the price with an expression which would have deterred any but the most reckless millionaire; he advocated a taxi, undertook to have one on hand at the right time, and effected a saving of some £5.

Often the *concierge*, in his role as fixer, simply invokes another of the hotel's services. In close association with the *concierge*, for instance, is the courier, historically the most interesting because he is rapidly dying out, though the use of the word as applied to an hotel servant who takes charge of travel arrangements is two centuries old.

Maxim Charrier—'Max the *chasseur*' to half a century of

Ritz clients—is the last staff courier in a Paris hotel. His only colleague—at the George V—died recently and was not replaced. Max is a stout, hearty sixty-seven and thinks he will give his job another couple of years and then retire. And then the race of courier will be extinct, for the modern type of courier, employed by a travel agent to conduct tourists, is not the same thing at all.

A courier like Max, although sixty clients a year still write or telegraph for his services, belongs to the days when air travel, and consequently 'travelling light', was, if not unknown, at least the exception. Max recalls travellers on the grand scale, like Mr Frederick Prince, the Chicago stockyard millionaire, who regularly travelled between America, Paris and his house at Pau in the South of France with ten servants and a hundred trunks and cases.

Mr Prince liked to travel by Wagon-Lit, and he was apt to change his mind about when he would travel. Max would meet him at Cherbourg and superintend the convoy to Paris. Then he would make the sleeper reservations and Mr Prince would decide to go south on a different date. It took all Max's skill and contacts to keep switching the multiple reservations and at last, when the decision was finally made, usually at short notice, to get the whole troupe and the mountain of baggage safely dispatched. 'Nowadays,' says Max, 'his son flies—with one suitcase.'

Max started at the Ritz when he was sixteen, in 1912, sweeping up in the basement and delivering packages to the rooms upstairs. He graduated to pageboy and thence to *chasseur*, opening car-doors, carrying luggage, calling taxis. In the First World War he was an interpreter with the American Army and he still proudly carries in his wallet a tattered certificate for this service.

He remained in uniform as *chasseur*, though changing to civilian clothes when he took on courier jobs, until the Thirties, when he became a full-time courier. He was a protégé of Olivier and has never forgotten, or ceased to apply, the precept Olivier gave him when he was a boy: 'Never say "no" when a client asks for something—even if it is the moon. You can always try, and anyhow there is plenty of time afterwards to explain that it was not possible.'

Sometimes his clients asked for services quite unconnected with travel. The Aga Khan used to get him to take his small son, Aly, walking in the Tuileries gardens. His duties for the Aga were so many and varied that Max says the best description of his function is 'almost a secretary'. He continued to serve Aly Khan when he was in Paris and eventually Aly took Max's son to work for him on his estate in Ireland, so that he might learn English.

Max has many American clients who have become friends. Bernard Baruch calls him his guardian angel; he always met Mr and Mrs Hutton and their small daughter Barbara at the ports, and he made their travelling arrangements so often that he automatically took charge of the grown-up Barbara's sometimes quite complicated travels, and has done so for thirty years now.

He 'receives' her from America, sees her on her way to Tangier after her stay in Paris, arranges her return in due course, and organises her off to her other home in Mexico as a regular annual pattern, although Miss Hutton no longer lives at the Ritz but has a Paris apartment of her own. Max is a fixed part of her life, and she of his.

Some clients, in the more leisurely and luxurious days, liked Max to accompany them on their travels. Whenever the American-born Baroness von Seidlitz went to London, Max went along. When the Cuban Colonel Caraf, an old Ritz frequenter, had to attend an international sugar conference he had Max meet him when he landed in France and escort him to Brussels and Berlin, taking charge of all the arrangements. The Maharajah of Kapurthala regularly went from Paris to Italy, and always had to be conducted by Max, who treasures a gold medal the Maharajah had struck specially for him. Once-crowned heads, such as Ferdinand of Rumania and Alfonso of Spain, also demanded the travel-nannying services of Max.

Once when the Aga Khan was upset about an international situation he wrote a letter and commissioned Max to deliver it personally to George V. When Max reached London he found the King was fulfilling a military engagement at Aldershot. He went there, delivered the letter, and was invited to stay to lunch—a memorable day in his life.

One American business man who has had Max make all his European travel arrangements for many years always announces his impending arrival by a letter addressed to Max at the Ritz as 'Director of Transportation'.

Nowadays Max's assignments tend to be relatively simple, by his standards. But in the past he was used to receiving very general instructions, usually from America; the client wanted to spend some time in Paris but also wanted to go to the Riviera and to Deauville at the appropriate times; would Max please arrange? The affection he inspired in his older clients shows now in such manifestations as long letters about his health (he was ill not long ago) from people he has not seen for years. One grateful client when parting from Max wrote something on a visiting card and gave it to him. It was an instruction to his representative in Brazil that at any time Max should require it he should be given a farm on the donor's estate. Max carries the card but has never taken up the offer.

After a lifetime as a courier, what does Max remember with most pride? He thought for only a moment and then told me. Immediately after the war an American millionaire he knew sent a truckload of food as a gift to the people of a Pyrenees village where he had a house. Max 'courier-ed' the consignment from port to destination—and got it through duty-free. Another treasure is a letter from a client whose wife had died. Max, deeply grieved, wrote a note of sympathy. The reply said, *inter alia*, 'The first thing we always looked for at Orly or Le Bourget was you. "Ah", we would say, "there's Max. All's well."' That is the ultimate tribute a conscientious courier could wish for.

*   *   *

The combination of Ritz decorum and the sort of services a good hotel feels bound to provide is not always easy to blend; a kiosk bedecked with theatre posters would be unthinkable. But between the Vendôme lobby and the *salon de thé*, sheltered in the curve of a staircase, there is a small, carved-wood counter which encloses Henri Galopin, who dispenses theatre tickets—and a variety of extra-mural information and advice to Ritz guests when called upon.

[201]

The surprising thing about Galopin is not his perfect command of English but his strident American accent. This is explained quite simply by the fact that he was born in Vermont of French parents, brought up in Washington, D.C., and came to France when his father was called up to the French Army in 1914. Galopin *père* was assigned as an interpreter to the Australian troops and was killed while serving in that capacity.

Henri joined the Ritz staff in 1916 and has been a Ritz institution ever since. 'A serious man who knows the theatre better than anybody, without having time to go,' a French newspaper wrote of him not long ago. (Galopin has the clipping in his desk.) 'At his modest *comptoir* on the Place Vendôme,' the eulogy continued, 'he does more for the prestige of France than all the press, radio and television put together.' This majestic claim stems from the fact that Galopin has a positive, at times even almost aggressive, approach to his job. He likes to judge new clients at a glance and decide what kind of show would appeal to them; and he is quite capable of overriding their preferences and dispatching them to the theatre he thinks appropriate. He is particularly impressive when—as happens surprisingly often—clients murmur about the price of the entertainments he offers. Then Galopin explodes, 'Too much for the Folies Bergère? Champagne too dear at the Lido? *Comparez!*' He then points out the prices for equivalent entertainments in New York, London, Madrid or Shanghai, while somehow conveying that there are no equivalents anyhow.

Galopin's amiable but sometimes high-handed methods extend to his friends. I approached him at a quiet time one evening for a chat and he was talking on the telephone. I signalled that I would wait until he was through but he said '*Moment*' into the receiver, placed it in the drawer of his counter, and shut the drawer. 'A friend,' he said with a deprecating intonation and a shrug, and we talked for a quarter of an hour; I was slightly distracted all the time by a fantasy-fear that the friend would suffocate.

Problems are Galopin's daily meat. Charles Ritz, who has known him for half a lifetime (they have a permanent deadpan joke in which M. Ritz, in his own semi-American English, tells

Galopin that he must do something about his terrible accent), says admiringly, 'He can find seats when nobody else can.' M. Ritz also acknowledges that when the new grill-room, L'Espadon, opened, its success was at least partly due to Galopin, quite unbidden, packaging his theatre tickets with instructions that the buyer could not do better than have supper in L'Espadon before the show.

Galopin's linguistic ability is formidable. When Marcel Achard's play *Patate* was running he could, he claims, translate *patate* into thirty languages. One day during the run of the same play, when seats were more than difficult to come by, a charming lady asked Galopin to help her. By his mysterious methods he procured two seats. 'Wonderful', she said. 'At last I can give pleasure to two of my dearest friends. My husband would like to help but he can't.' Only then did Galopin discover that the lady was Mme Achard.

Galopin particularly treasures incidents the humour of which he was unable to share at the time. Soon after the Liberation a South American lady arrived and asked Galopin what was going on in Paris. '*The Brothers Karamazov* at the Atelier', Galopin suggested. 'Ah, I'm so glad they're back too,' she said.

Pretentiousness punctured is his favourite theme. There was the gushing lady who came to his desk one day with a friend and said, 'What was the play in which Louis Jouvet created the role of Sodom—or was it Gomorrah? I remember it so well. . . .'

An Egyptian for whom Galopin had performed feats of ticket-procuring over the years arrived one evening en route for America. 'I have a seat on a plane tonight', he said 'but I'll stay over if you can get me a seat for *Le Petit Café* at the Antoine.' Galopin made some calls, then shook his head. 'No seats,' he said. Later one of Galopin's assistant miracle-workers came on the telephone with the news that one *strapontin* (or aisle jump-seat) was available. Galopin figured that the Egyptian would have retired to the bar to await his plane time. He rang through and his guess was right. 'No', said the Egyptian, 'I don't want a *strapontin*. I'll fly tonight.' Galopin was not going to let his minor triumph be treated like that. 'Why don't you be like other people for once?'

he said. 'What's wrong with a *strapontin* if you really want to see
the play? Miss your plane.' The Egyptian surrendered; the
plane was the one which crashed killing France's then top-rating
boxing star, Marcel Cerdan, and Ginette Neveu, the famous
violinist.

There has only been one interruption in Galopin's long reign
in his pulpit-like headquarters and though he can smile about it
now it was distinctly unpleasant at the time. When the Germans
were in occupation one of the most imperious who stayed at the
Ritz was Sauckel, who was in charge of the disposition of French
man-power. The staircase in the lee of which Galopin operates
leads to the apartments Sauckel occupied. When he and his
entourage went up the stairs Galopin studiously paid no attention.
One night Sauckel stopped and ordered Galopin to stand up
when he went by. Galopin refused. He was sent to work in the
Renault factory for a year. He showed me his factory identity
card. I remarked that in the photograph he seemed much slimmer
than he is now. Galopin smiled. 'I had to be. When you'—he
meant the Royal Air Force—'came over one had to be able to run
fast.'

Inevitably Galopin has a wide circle of friends and acquain-
tances among the Ritz guests and not all the conversations conducted at his counter concern theatre seats. There was a lady who
confided in him that she wanted to have a coffee ice with her tea,
but could he ensure for her that the ice-cream would be made
with decaffeinated coffee?

While he finds that over the years people, in their relations
with hotel servants, have become 'more human' he has to be
wary of those who are still something less than democratic. He
had an awkward moment with a high-born Englishwoman who
walked past the desk as he emitted one of his loud 'hellos' on the
telephone. Without thinking she said 'Hello', walked on a pace
or two, then turned back and said indignantly 'How dare you say
hello to me?'

One of the telephones with which Galopin constantly juggles
as he operates his network of contacts is a curious engraved brass
affair, more like a hollow shoehorn than a telephone. He swears

by its efficiency, regards it as something of a lucky charm, and proudly announces that in 1964 it will celebrate its fiftieth anniversary of continuous use.

Galopin's accent remains a cause of occasional confusion. 'There was an American,' he recalls, 'you know, a patriot, who asked me one day where I got my accent. I explained I was born in America. "Then you're American", he said. "You're more American than any naturalised American who has lived there eighty years. You're American-*born*." I tried to shrug it off and say I was really French on account of my parentage and, what's more, I *feel* French, but he interrupted me, held up his hand and said, "Enough. You are a traitor to your country", and hit me over the head with his cane.'

Like almost every old servant of the Ritz, Galopin has his favourite story of minor, amiable eccentricity on the part of the clientele. His concerns the elderly Lady X, who spent years in the hotel and travelled several times a day in the lift alongside Galopin's desk. On entering the vintage, one-speed lift she never failed to put her hand on the liftboy's shoulder and say, 'Not too fast'.

*　　*　　*

If you told a Ritz habitué that Harry Burrer had recently retired after half a century at the hotel he might well pucker his brow and wonder how he could have failed to know someone who had been around so long. But if you told him that Emile, the barber, had retired, the reaction would be quite different. M. Burrer was professionally 'Emile' throughout his long working life (it is at once mysterious and obvious that a *coiffeur* just cannot be called Harry) and he was one of the best-known figures at the Ritz; for many men scattered about the world it will be difficult to imagine the little barber shop, opposite the lift on the first floor, without the lined, friendly face of Emile presiding over the first chair inside the door.

Emile, like Maurice, the *chef des caves*, had only one predecessor in the Ritz's history; the first barber, who opened his shop with the hotel in 1898, was Marius Combes, another famous Ritz character in his time, and Emile came as his assistant in 1913. The following year he joined the French Army (he is Alsatian by birth) and after he returned in 1920 his service with the Ritz was continuous till the end of 1962.

Originally Emile's work in the hotel was mostly for ladies. He had a staff of three hairdressers and two manicurists. One of the most revolutionary changes in Emile's time is that nowadays young men are preferred as *coiffeurs*. When Emile was young, only older men were thought suitable to dress ladies' hair; when he was twenty he was told by his boss that he was too young and that he might disguise his youth by growing a beard. If asked his age, he said he was twenty-five, which apparently made a great difference. When he went to England in 1911 at the time of the coronation of George V he was wearing his beard; one day a small boy in the street made a face and brayed a goat-like 'Me-e-eh' at him. Emile at once shaved off the beard, never to grow it again.

Barbers have a generic reputation as talkers, and particularly as gossips, but like all generalisations this is not always true and in fact many barbers find themselves on the receiving end of far more gossip, off-the-record information, scandal and confidences than they ever utter. Indeed as the Ritz barber Emile soon decided to be a model of discretion. He declared his attitude quite early in his career, and it was to a man who was to be a customer and friend for the rest of his life.

One day the late Aga Khan asked Emile a question to answer which truthfully would have been, in Emile's judgment, to pass on gossip. He replied politely that he would no more answer the question than he would tell other people things told to him by the Aga Khan. The Prince thought about this for a moment, then turned and shook Emile's hand in approval. From then on he confided in Emile.

Whenever the Aga Khan was in Paris members of the Ismaeli Muslim community, of which he was spiritual head, came to the Ritz with their problems and requests, or simply to pay homage to their leader, the descendant of the Prophet. At first the order was that they should be admitted freely and Emile recalls picking his way along the corridor to the Aga Khan's suite, stepping over prostrate Ismaelis lying face down with their shoes off. The Aga Khan eventually had to modify his open-audience policy and see the faithful by appointment only.

Emile only once saw the Aga Khan badly rattled. A woman had obtained an interview with him and then revealed her real purpose: she had heard that in the Aga's country there was a poison which was entirely untraceable. Would the Aga please help her to obtain some as she needed it 'for domestic reasons'? When Emile arrived to shave His Highness he was giving vehement orders that this woman should never again be admitted to his presence.

A few days before the Aga Khan died he asked for Emile to fly from Paris to Geneva to shave him. He did so and no sooner had he returned to Paris than another call came, but this time the doctors said it was too late, and the Aga died two days later.

It is Emile's belief that for some inexplicable reason there are people of both sexes who think a barber or *coiffeur* in attendance upon them is blind and deaf, or, by an even more extraordinary feat of the imagination, regard him as invisible. But for a decision he made early in his career, Emile says, he is sure he would have been less successful and less happy. He decided that he must be unshockable. This undoubtedly became easier with the passage of time, but in his early days it cost him considerable effort.

It should be remembered, of course, that ninety-nine in a hundred of Emile's customers were sober, law-abiding, normal citizens, but when a man looks back over a long life it is the colourful and off-beat things which tend to light up in the memory; also, Emile likes to chuckle as he reminisces, and human oddity and foible have always amused him in his role of privileged observer.

There was, for instance, a Ritz resident who liked to be shaved twice a day in his suite and liked to have a drink at the same time, but he could not bear to drink alone. He insisted that the barber join him and, though a reasonably abstemious man, Emile admits he enjoyed the morning glass of champagne and the evening whisky-and-soda.

Once in a while Emile rebelled, not from shock but from a hurt

to his pride which he would not tolerate. Many years ago there
was a distinguished international lawyer who was a monumental
drinker, and also extremely irascible. He drank a bottle of brandy
between getting up and noon, two bottles of champagne in the
course of the day, and switched back to brandy in the evening.
Not surprisingly he was often less than sober when Emile
attended him.

One day when Emile finished shaving him he began to readjust
his tie, then stopped and announced loudly that he had been
robbed; his valuable tiepin was missing. Emile started to look for
it, but the lawyer, jumping to most unlawyerlike conclusions,
immediately accused Emile of stealing it. Emile said nothing but
reached down into the folds of the man's waistcoat where the
tiepin had fallen, handed it to him, and said, 'Now go to hell,'
and walked out.

The only other time he can recall a sharp issue with a customer
was when he found a Russian guest beating a servant with a stick.
Emile stopped him, but the Russian explained that the servant
was drunk. Even so, Emile said, and read the astonished Russian
a lecture on humane behaviour. Emile recalls this incident vividly
over the years because he realised that it had never occurred to the
Russian that there was anything wrong or even criticisable about
beating a servant.

The pre-First-World-War Russians who frequented the Ritz
were a memorable lot so far as behaviour was concerned. Emile
once went into a Russian prince's suite on a New Year's morning
to find the floor thickly strewn with money and the Prince in the
bath with his top-hat on. With a wide and princely gesture he
indicated the money and shouted, 'Help yourself'.

One barbering story which amuses Emile over the years did not
directly involve him. A Russian grand duke telephoned M.
Auzello from Cannes on a Friday and announced that he would be
arriving next day and wanted 'his usual apartment'. The suite in
question was occupied until the Saturday night, so Auzello
arranged for the Grand Duke to be accommodated at the neighbouring Hotel Vendôme for one night. On the Sunday morning
the Grand Duke telephoned the Ritz and demanded Emile. It was

pointed out that Emile did not work on Sundays. This quibble did not impress the Grand Duke, who merely said, 'Send for him'. A taxi was dispatched to fetch Emile from his home, but he had gone away to the country. By the joint efforts of the Ritz and Vendôme managements a barber was at last found, but he was a man who had practised only ladies' hairdressing for years and he had none of the necessary tools of the trade. Auzello sent round his own razor, shaving soap and brush and thought the problem solved.

But the barber was out of practice and he began to shave the Grand Duke with short, tentative strokes. Twice the Grand Duke roared, 'Not like that' and demonstrated how he liked to be shaved. (It may well be asked at this point why he did not go ahead and do the job himself: no answer is available.) But the Grand Duke was still not satisfied, and his never slow temper was steadily rising. After another interruption, the barber attempted an answer, beginning, 'Sir . . .' 'Call me monseigneur,' roared the Grand Duke. That was the last straw. The barber packed up and said firmly, 'You can get yourself shaved by the Devil himself but not by me,' and left. He had completed shaving one side of the imperial face; the other side had a heavy growth of beard. The Grand Duke spent the day half-shaved and kept no social engagements.

Emile for many years dressed the hair of Queen Marie of Rumania when she was at the Ritz. He had nothing but the most amiable dealings with her personally, but her entourage gave him trouble occasionally because they were so tight-fisted about money. Once when Emile was off duty and at home on a Sunday he was asked to come to the hotel and dress the Queen's hair for a late function she was to attend. He did so, working from ten o'clock until nearly midnight. When he presented the bill the lady-in-waiting protested that it was much too high. He was a servant of the hotel, she said, and the hotel charges were so and so. Emile pointed out that he had come from home by taxi, that he had been unable to use theatre seats he had bought for that night, and that he had to take a double-fare taxi home. There were long protestations, but Emile would not budge. At last the lady-in-waiting asked if he would accept a cut in his bill if she arranged for him to be given a Rumanian decoration. Emile, unimpressed, held out for cash, and won.

The stringency of the Rumanian court economy seems to have stemmed from the King, Ferdinand. He did not like to pay a barber regularly to trim his beard and carried his own clippers. Once he asked Emile to buy him new clippers. Emile did so and when he delivered them the King gave him the old ones, apparently considering this a fair exchange. Emile pointed out that the old clippers were useless and worthless. The King thought this unreasonable and in the end his best offer was the old clippers plus five francs—then about four shillings. Emile did not deign to argue.

There was another Middle European royalty who asked Emile why she couldn't have a discount on his charges as she heard film stars did. Emile said certainly she could have a discount, provided she did not mind her photograph being used for advertising—as the film stars photographs were. She reluctantly agreed to pay the full price.

A client of Emile's for many years was one of the Middle Eastern oil kings, whose eccentricities were innumerable. Like many very rich men, he had a horror of being overcharged or exploited. He had his hair trimmed regularly and each time he would take out his watch and lay it on the dressing table. Then he would tell Emile sternly that his hair must be cut in exactly half-an-hour, and he was prepared to pay only on a time basis. Emile says the only problem was how to make a ten-minute job last thirty to satisfy the client.

The same multi-millionaire once explained to Emile why he was so careful over small amounts of money. He would study his bills scrupulously, checking the items and the arithmetic, and was delighted if he could find a five-franc error. The five francs, he explained, was not the point; by spotting the error or overcharge he would make people be very careful in future and realise that he was not a man who could be easily robbed.

Among the other eccentricities of this millionaire was that he never went to the theatre because of a fear of fire. He had two blood analyses made every month by different doctors so that he could compare them. One piece of unsolicited advice he once gave to Emile was: 'Always give your girl-friends small jewels— pretty but small. If you give them big ones, they may sell them and leave you.'

*   *   *

Ironic situations always appealed to Emile. There was a millionaire who went out every morning and bought a quarter of a pound of butter and a bottle of mineral water because they were cheaper in the shops than in the hotel. Meanwhile his wife was having her hair done by Emile, usually with an expensive beauty treatment at the same time.

Once when Paderewski, the great pianist and Prime Minister of Poland, was staying at the Ritz Emile was sent for to cut his hair. Emile was surprised, as he had never been called upon before. When he arrived at the suite he was met by Madame Paderewski, who looked at him suspiciously. 'What do you want?' she demanded. Emile explained; Madame Paderewski seized the scissors from his hand, sat her celebrated husband in a chair, flattened his hair down both sides and ran the scissors swiftly round the perimeter. 'Now you may go,' she said to Emile, handing back the scissors. Paderewski later admitted that this was how his hair was usually cut, but he had wanted a professional cut for a change.

When the Germans were in occupation an anxious captain who was having his hair cut by Emile whispered that he wanted to speak to him privately. They went outside the barber shop and the German, very embarrassed, confided that his general was demanding what are usually and simply known as 'feelthy pictures', and the aide had no idea where to find them. His job was at stake. Emile must help.

Emile refused abruptly and turned back to his shop. The captain clutched desperately at his arm. 'I can get you food,' he said. 'All the things you can't get.'

That, in the exigencies of war, made Emile think again. He said he would see what he could do. In fact he had no idea where to start, but he asked around and was at last directed to a small back-street shop. The woman who ran it at first denied that she did any such trade. She was obviously frightened. Emile put the situation frankly to her. If she had such things why shouldn't she sell them and get food into the bargain? Emile was determined to keep out of the transaction, so he simply introduced the captain to the shop. He feels sure the captain, and his general, must have been satisfied because he had a useful supply of butter as his reward for some time afterwards.

Emile once shaved Göring—a tempting situation for any Frenchman. What mystified Emile about this summons was that he knew that Göring had his own valet-barber in attendance. However, he went along to the suite and to his surprise found a very quiet, subdued, almost nervous man where he had expected the opposite. They barely exchanged a word. He discovered the explanation later. Driving into Paris from Versailles the previous night Göring had had a bomb thrown at his car; he had had a narrow escape and his valet had been wounded.

Göring had three nephews on his staff. All of them came to Emile's shop. One of them came in looking exceptionally cheerful the day the Allied Forces landed in Normandy. Emile asked him why he was so happy. 'Because at last there will be a battle,' was the reply, 'and therefore a winner and a loser—and if I survive I can go home.' Emile made no comment. The German sighed and added, 'I hope Paris is not damaged. My dearest wish is to bring my wife and children here when the war is over and show them the most beautiful city in the world.' Emile never saw or heard of him again.

EPILOGUE

THE TWENTIETH CENTURY so far has had more distinct epochs—and more social revolution—than most centuries have packed into sixty-three years. Considering the nature and degree of change that has gone on around it, the Ritz's most remarkable feat is surely to have achieved continuity without ossification; for all its varied history, it is a living hotel and not a museum.

When it opened, Victoria was on the throne of England and Victorian society and its equivalent elsewhere seemed immutable. It throve in the Edwardian era when the boundaries and composition of 'society' changed vastly; it was an ornament and rendezvous of the very different life of 'society' in the Twenties. It unwillingly housed the Nazi hierarchy of the Second World War in an occupied Paris which, at one time, only optimists believed was likely ever to recover its former glory. But it emerged, put its liberated house in order, and resumed its accustomed way.

It has been a home for the busy rich, like the early South African and American millionaires, and for the idle rich; it has leant for its support on a clientele ranging from royalty to what (however rich they may be) must realistically be called tourists.

Only a handful of men have been responsible for its direction over the years, dedicated to maintaining the standards of one man in a world constantly moving farther and farther away from the world he knew and for which he catered. How unreal and high-flown now seem the words of Henry Higgins, the English lawyer who was César's backer, at the time of the hotel's opening: 'Kings and princes will be jealous of you, Ritz. You are going to teach the world how to live.' No doubt he was serious and sincere; his 'world' was a small and settled community. Now the kings and the princes are fewer and if the world has not learned to 'live' in the Ritz sense a great many more people can now enjoy some of the refinements and luxuries which Ritz provided for the few.

And the Ritz goes on. From the insider's viewpoint, as Claude Auzello put it, it is 'an amusing life, but you do not make much money'. From the customer's point of view, it is an oasis in a crowded, clangorous and confused world. What Marcel Proust said of it is still true. Nobody jostles you.